TWO AGAINST THE ICE

AMUNDSEN AND ELLSWORTH

THEODORE K. MASON

Illustrated with photographs and maps

TWO AGAINST THE ICE

AMUNDSEN AND ELLSWORTH

DODD, MEAD & COMPANY · New York

ILLUSTRATIONS COURTESY OF:

Alexander Turnbull Library, 61, 72; American Museum of Natural History, 167, 173, 180–181; Library of Congress, 8, 14, 24, 31, 40–41, 50, 51, 53, 54, 56, 59, 60, 64, 67, 68–69, 73, 74, 75, 76, 89, 91, 93, 112, 115, 116, 118, 119, 121, 122, 123, 125, 126, 128, 130, 135 *top,* 138, 141, 143, 145, 156, 177; Theodore K. Mason, 27, 36, 66, 70 *top,* 85, 95, 133, 169, 175; National Archives, 151; National Portrait Gallery, London, 39; Norsk Sjøfartsmuseum, 34, (from *Fifteen Months in the Antarctic*) 28, 30, (from *My Life as an Explorer*) 83, (from *Northeast Passage*) 86, (from *Northwest Passage*) 43, 45, 46, 49, (from *Our Polar Flight*) 10, 101, 106–107, 110; Norwegian Information Service, 17, 80, 111, 146, 157; Private collection of Marion Plotkin, 135 *bottom,* 148, 187; Paul Ratajczak, *title page;* Paul Ratajczak after "FR," Boy Scouts of America, 99; Scott Polar Research Institute, 57, 63, 70 *bottom,* 78, 79; U.S. Navy, 13, 160, 164, 171, 179; Jakob Vaage, Oslo, 22.

1   2   3   4   5   6   7   8   9   10

Library of Congress Cataloging in Publication Data

Mason, Theodore K.
  Two against the ice, Amundsen and Ellsworth.

  Bibliography: p.
  Includes index.
  1. Amundsen, Roald, 1872–1928. 2. Ellsworth,
Lincoln, 1880–1951. 3. Polar regions—
Discovery and exploration. 4. Explorers—
Norway—Biography. 5. Explorers—United States
—Biography. I. Title.
G585.A6M34   1982   919.8′04′0922 [B]   82-45383
ISBN 0-396-08092-8

ACKNOWLEDGMENTS

The author wishes to thank the following for their assistance in gathering materials for this book:

Alexander Turnbull Library, Wellington, New Zealand
Boy Scouts of America
National Archives, Washington, D.C.
National Portrait Gallery, London
New York Public Library
Norwegian Information Service, New York
Office of Information, Department of the Navy, Washington, D.C.
Polar Information Service, National Science Foundation, Washington, D.C.
Scott Polar Research Institute, Cambridge, England
United States Department of the Interior, National Park Service, Golden Gate National Recreation Area, San Francisco
Universitetets Etnografiske Museum, Oslo
Jakob Vaage, Oslo

and with special thanks to:

Rosemary Casey, Dodd, Mead, & Company, New York
Jerry Kerns, the Library of Congress, Washington, D.C.
Else Marie Thorstvedt, Norsk Sjøfartsmuseum, Oslo
William Kuehl, New York
Marion Plotkin, Linden, New Jersey
Paul Ratajczak, New York

CONTENTS

Roald Amundsen, aged forty-eight

1

TWO POLAR PIONEERS

Their predicament appeared hopeless. Trapped with four companions in the jaws of the Arctic ice pack, Roald Amundsen and Lincoln Ellsworth were on their first expedition together. Their attempt to become the first to fly over the top of the world was a daring adventure. Everyone feared it would end in disaster.

After taking off from Spitsbergen (now Svalbard), they had put down by mistake 165 miles from their objective, the North Pole. From the air, the floating fragments of ice had appeared to be welded together in a single flat sheet. The vast canopy seemed to cover the ocean, except for pools of water that looked like oases in a desert and channels that snaked through the whiteness like black sidewinders.

But the ice proved to be deceptive. Up close it was ridged with wall-like hummocks and jumbled with giant blocks of ice tossed up by the pressure of the moving pack. Above the chaos, the sun blazed twenty-four hours a day, turning the scene into a glare of blue and white, and burning their skins black.

One of their two seaplanes was damaged beyond repair, the other beached like a whale among the drifting ice floes. Their food was running out. They were at the mercy of currents that might carry them south where warmer temperatures would melt the ice from under them. Rescue seemed impossible. They had no radio. No one knew where, in the vast, unknown region, to start searching for them. In fact, the world had given them up as lost.

They had two options. They could stay with the operable plane, or they could make a desperate attempt to reach the Greenland coast, the nearest land.

One of the Dornier-Wal seaplanes, N-24, of the Amundsen-Ells-worth Polar flight, stranded on the Arctic ice pack

Most of the crew wanted to "finish on their feet," but they feared that the trek across 340 miles of ice pack would be impossible.

"It *can* be done," Roald Amundsen assured them, although the Norwegian leader knew it would probably be a death march.

Before deserting the plane, however, Amundsen was determined to make a supreme effort to get it into the air. The world's greatest living explorer wasn't the type to be defeated by adversity. He had been in some seemingly inescapable scrapes before. If anybody could save them, Amundsen could.

Amundsen's reputation as an explorer was also at stake. His previous enterprise, the *Maud* Expedition, had been a disaster. Twice he had nearly been killed. His health was such that doctors had warned him that he wouldn't survive another expedition. His countrymen considered him to be dishonest. He was bankrupt, lonely, and embittered.

In the fall of 1924, seven months before the flight to the North Pole, the fallen hero had traveled to the United States to lecture and write newspaper articles. He'd brought with him his most treasured belongings. If he couldn't raise enough money to buy two seaplanes for a transarctic flight, he intended to retire to Maudheim, the cabin he had built at Wainwright, Alaska, at the end of the *Maud* saga.

He nearly retired to Alaska. The American public, like the Norwegians in 1924, had lost interest in polar exploration. Few were intrigued by the future of aircraft in polar work. Amundsen's newspaper articles didn't earn him much toward paying off his debts. His lecture tour was close to a financial failure.

Only an obscure newspaper article announced his arrival in New York City that October. But it was enough to catch the attention of Lincoln Ellsworth. Amundsen had been one of the boyhood heroes of Ellsworth, who had recently returned from leading his own first expedition—a topographical survey across the Peruvian Andes.

For ten years Ellsworth had wanted to undertake an Arctic

11

expedition, but his wealthy father steadfastly refused to back such a dangerous enterprise. In Amundsen, Ellsworth saw his chance, although he'd been turned down by the Norwegian six years earlier, when he begged to be included in the *Maud* Expedition.

Mustering his courage, Ellsworth telephoned Amundsen's New York hotel room and asked him for an hour of his time. "I met you several years ago in France during the war," he explained.

Amundsen was in no mood to receive someone he had met only briefly. But then the caller added, "I am an amateur interested in exploration, and I might be able to supply some money for another expedition." Those were the magic words. Amundsen, who had spent most of his career fighting for financial support, could hardly refuse to see a man with money to spend.

Ellsworth offered to help buy two seaplanes for the transarctic flight if he could share the command. The only hitch was convincing his iron-willed father to give them the money.

Amundsen was recharged with hope, although he didn't realize what a long shot it was. As the two talked on through dinner, he seemed to become younger. Ellsworth left the hotel that night with his "head in the stars."

After much pleading, Ellsworth finally convinced his father to meet Amundsen. When they were introduced, Ellsworth wrote that the two older men sat down eyeing each other suspiciously—"the grim, old, white-faced financier facing the gray, bald but vigorous, weather-beaten old Viking!"

"I suppose you have something to tell me, Captain Amundsen?" James Ellsworth asked.

"What do you want to know?"

"About your experiences. What this business is like."

In high-pitched, heavily accented English, Amundsen told of his past explorations and made a favorable impression. He won over the elder Ellsworth, who offered to back the venture with $85,000, which was the cost of the seaplanes. To this Lincoln

Lincoln Ellsworth, aged fifty-three

added another $10,000 by telling his father's lawyer that it was for parachutes.

But on the following day, when the three men met again, James Ellsworth balked. The contract lay on the table like the "articles of surrender" to his son.

James Ellsworth, Lincoln's father

"Lincoln," the old man said, "if I give this money, will you promise me never to touch tobacco again?"

His 44-year-old son reluctantly agreed. He would have agreed to just about anything. The contract was signed. As a way of thanking him, Amundsen presented the financier with the binoculars he had used during his conquests of the Northwest Passage and the South Pole.

But Lincoln didn't feel compelled to keep his promise about smoking because he had been coerced into the agreement and because his father tried to renege on the deal. The old man sent for Matt Henson, the Black man who had accompanied Robert Peary to the North Pole. Henson had told reporters that he thought the airplane expedition was suicidal.

"Can an airplane reach the North Pole?" James Ellsworth demanded.

"Absolutely not. There is nothing at the North Pole but howling blizzards and ice piled up like mountains," Henson replied.

Lincoln rebutted that every book written on the subject, including Peary's, described the Arctic as calm, foggy, and having equable conditions during the summer. He also reminded his father that Peary had predicted the conquest of the Arctic by air.

Nevertheless, James Ellsworth continued his campaign to keep his son from accompanying Amundsen. He even went so far as to telephone the White House in an attempt to have Lincoln's passport canceled. Although considerable inheritance was at stake, Lincoln wrote that he would have risked his soul to go on the flight with Amundsen. In the battle of wills, Lincoln eventually won, probably because his sister, Clare, interceded on his behalf, even though she, too, believed he was going to his death.

Angered by his defeat, James Ellsworth used the excuse of ill health to avoid seeing Lincoln off when he left to join the expedition. It was an unfortunate act of stubbornness on the part of a father who would never see his son again.

"Father was no more yielding than a granite crag," Ellsworth said in his autobiography.

Amundsen had had much the same type of father—a stern sea captain and shipowner. Both fathers were successful, self-made men. Their word was law, even though they were gone from home most of the time. Amundsen's father was usually at sea, where he died when Roald was fourteen. When Ellsworth was eight, his mother died of pneumonia and his father sent him away to be taken care of by his grandmother on an Ohio farm.

Both fathers were men of position and gave their sons the advantages of the upper reaches of society, including private schools, although James Ellsworth was far the wealthier of the two.

The two boys were quiet types who decided at an early age to become explorers. Amundsen was fascinated by stories of John

Franklin and Fridtjof Nansen. Ellsworth thrilled to the exploits of Nansen, Peary, Theodore Roosevelt, and Amundsen himself, although his greatest hero was Wyatt Earp.

Ellsworth particularly admired Earp because the marshall was described in the book *Tombstone* as having "altered the course of Western history by his domination over men and events." Ellsworth got in touch with the widowed Mrs. Earp and enjoyed hearing stories of her husband. Earp was the type of tough hero Ellsworth would have liked to have been, but wasn't; one of his later colleagues described him as "lovable," although somewhat vain and petulant. Ellsworth was an admitted sentimentalist, and collected souvenirs.

Both Amundsen and Ellsworth, as fledgling frontiersmen, had found the classroom to be a prison. Neither did well, but both managed to gain university entrance. To please his mother, Amundsen began to study medicine. He flunked his first-year exams. Not wanting anyone to know of his failure, he kept it a secret all of his life. When his mother died, he happily escaped to pursue his career as a polar explorer.

Ellsworth was dropped by Yale University after his first year because of a poor academic record. He was more interested in reading about Teddy Roosevelt's adventures as a sheriff single-handedly rounding up desperadoes. Ellsworth also tried Columbia University, where he studied mineralogy and mining. But he quickly left during the second-year final exams when he had a chance to join the Canadian Pacific Railway.

Their poor academic showings, however, didn't mean that Amundsen and Ellsworth were incapable of learning. They were exceptionally adept at subjects they were interested in or needed to further their careers. Amundsen, for instance, learned terrestrial magnetism in Germany to give his navigation of the Northwest Passage a scientific mission and thereby gained the backing of the scientific community.

Surprisingly, neither youth was physically equipped to lead a rigorous life. Both had poor eyesight, a fact Amundsen con-

"Svartskog"—home of Roald Amundsen near Oslo, Norway

cealed by never wearing his glasses in public. Both set out to toughen their bodies, particularly Amundsen, who was considered a freak when he slept with his window open during the Norwegian winter. Even though he didn't like football, he played the game to improve his physical condition. His love was long skiing jaunts. As a result, doctors were so amazed by his physique when they examined him for his military duty that they didn't bother to check his eyes. If they had, he would have been rejected as unfit, which would have devastated his pride.

As a youth, Ellsworth was a weakling, timid, and anemic. He, too, had to build up his body. Although he played tennis and cycled, his forte was long distance running. He started wrestling when he became an adult and claimed at the age of thirty that he could take on a professional. In later life he liked to take long walks, as did Amundsen.

Both men were infected with the pioneering spirit. They were as uncomfortable in civilization as they were in the classroom. Cities seemed to overwhelm them. They wanted to be out under the sky, finding something nobody else had found before, seeing what had not been seen. When Amundsen departed on an expedition, he liked to slip away at midnight and avoid noisy crowds. (Of course, he and Ellsworth wanted to be cheered home as heroes when the venture was over.)

Ellsworth hated everything that hinted of ease and luxury—much to the dismay of his father who had worked to make his son comfortable for life. Ellsworth wanted "to battle for his life, for his food, and for warmth," his sister wrote. The same was said of Amundsen, who sailed on the *Belgica* to Antarctica in 1897. While his shipmates, trapped in the ice pack, were venting their frustrations, Amundsen was depicted in the ship's magazine as an ascetic-looking figure, saying, "Yes, sir. I love it!" Both Amundsen and Ellsworth delighted in sacrifice and self-denial.

The two explorers were described as vain. Both enjoyed dressing well, whether in ordinary suits or Eskimo furs. Both had a boyish nature. In the lovable Ellsworth, this was readily apparent. Years of persecution and betrayal had forced Amundsen to conceal his true self, as well as his gusto for life, behind a chilly reserve. Ellsworth was one of the few allowed to see behind that façade. Once Amundsen's confidence was won, Ellsworth said of him, "Nobody was warmer hearted, no boy could frolic more joyously than Amundsen in his fifties."

The glittering white expanse of the polar regions appeared to be the true love of both men. Amundsen never married. He had only one brief romantic affair, as far as anyone knows. Ellsworth was fifty-three before he took marriage vows.

Born in New York City, the first Amundsen-Ellsworth expedition was an ideal partnership. Amundsen gave his new American friend the benefit of his experience and the opportunity to realize his ambitions. Ellsworth provided the money and the respect Amundsen desperately needed. They were well suited to one another and got on remarkably well. Ellsworth worshipped Amundsen as a hero; Amundsen beamed in the glow of admiration. They became a team, two polar pioneers in search of the unknown. Most people, however, deemed them to be a pair of suicidal nuts.

MISSING SKIERS

Amundsen seemed bent on self-destruction from the time of his first attempt at exploring. After finishing a required short stint in the army, he decided to tackle the Hardangervidda, a forbidding mountain plateau in central Norway. Largely unknown, the high country had been crossed only once before during the winter.

He tried once with two companions and failed miserably. After spending a month in preparation, the embarrassed young

Viking couldn't even get his skis to work properly. The terrain where they started was too rough for skiing.

Undaunted, Amundsen tried again. This time he took his brother Leon with him. The crossing should have taken a week. When nothing had been heard from the brothers after two weeks, an alarm was raised. MISSING SKIERS! headlined newspapers in Christiania (now Oslo). As the days passed, the two were given up as lost. Amundsen had made his debut.

The most difficult aspect of the 100-mile trek involved skiing over forty miles of windswept plateau from a remote farm on the eastern side to one near the western coast. Visibility was poor due to snow, overcast skies, and the short daylight hours which at that time of year are like twilight.

Midway across the plateau, the brothers arrived at a deserted hut, used by the Lapps during the summer. A blizzard trapped them there. Luckily they had shelter, and found an abandoned sack of rye flour, which they made into a nasty-tasting porridge in order to save their scant rations.

After pressing on, the two young men were engulfed by another storm. Losing their bearings, they wandered around aimlessly. Because they hadn't brought along a tent or a stove, they were forced to camp in the open that night, without the benefit of anything hot to eat or drink. The next morning, they woke to discover that their provision bag had disappeared without a trace. Amundsen was never able to explain the mysterious loss. Was it due to the wind? Was it wolverines?

Whatever the explanation, the brothers were in trouble. They might starve or freeze to death unless they could reach food and shelter quickly. Setting forth on their skis, they hoped to gain the western edge of the plateau by nightfall. But it soon began to snow so heavily that they couldn't see more than a few feet ahead. They decided it was safer to retreat. Unknown to them until later, they were within yards of their destination when they turned back.

The novice explorers managed several miles before it became

Amundsen (right) with Laurentius Urdahl (left) and Wilhelm Holst, before an attempt to cross the Hardangervidda, 1893

too dark to travel farther. With no shelter available, they sought protection on the lee side of a small peak. Roald gouged a hole in the snow and climbed in headfirst, pulling his sleeping bag in after him. Leon, however, was too exhausted to do any digging and sacked out a short distance away. A simple tent would have seemed like a palace then, but they had none.

When Roald woke, he discovered that falling snow had covered him and then frozen, entombing him in a block of ice. He struggled and shouted until he realized he couldn't breathe properly. Slowly, he began to slip into unconsciousness, an extremely dangerous predicament because sleep always precedes freezing in such situations.

Fortunately Leon found his brother's feet sticking out of the snow. Using his ski pole, he dug frantically until he managed to extricate the young man who one day would conquer the frozen ends of the earth.

Although it was still dark and they were exhausted, they decided to get underway, with only the stars to guide them. They had marched for two hours when Leon, who was leading, suddenly disappeared. The fast-thinking Roald flattened himself on the snow. After a few moments, he heard Leon's voice.

"Don't move! I have dropped over a precipice!"

Despite the thirty-foot drop, Leon was only shaken up. The rolled-up sleeping bag on his back had cushioned his fall. Once he'd been rescued, the two rested and traveled on at daylight, with increasing hunger compounding their exhaustion. They had been without food for six days, except for the meager porridge they had made in the Lapp hut. Water, which they drank from small unfrozen lakes along the way, was the only sustenance that enabled them to keep going.

Their spirits picked up at nightfall when they found a shanty filled with hay. Surely civilization was near, they believed, as they burrowed into the straw. In the morning, while looking around, Roald encountered a farmer who fled, thinking he had seen a ghost. The ordeal had left Roald haggard and gaunt, with a scraggly beard and greenish-yellow skin. His eyes and cheeks seemed gouged out.

On the other side of the Atlantic, meanwhile, Amundsen's future partner was suffering the rigors of boarding school. Lincoln Ellsworth felt incarcerated at school. To him, a happy episode was getting pneumonia because assignments couldn't follow him into the infirmary, and afterward he was sent home to convalesce. No one would have believed that Ellsworth would one day become a rugged polar explorer.

Amundsen, about the time of the Belgica *Expedition*

3

TRAPPED IN THE ANTARCTIC

The Hardangervidda served as Amundsen's primer. He soon was to learn another, more dangerous lesson about exploring when he signed on the *Belgica* Expedition as third mate.

The Belgian leader, Lieutenant Adrien de Gerlache, intended to land with a small shore party on the Victoria Land Coast of Antarctica and become the first to winter on the continent. His scientific mission: to travel inland and survey the South Magnetic Pole. Amundsen was to be in De Gerlache's select but untried group. From working on Arctic sealing ships, Roald had some polar experience. But the only pro in the group was Dr. Frederick Cook, the ship's doctor, from Brooklyn, New York. He had been with Robert Peary on his trip to Greenland five years earlier. Amundsen took immediate interest in him.

The *Belgica* sailed south on August 23, 1897, on what became one of the great Antarctic sagas. By January the trailblazers were dodging icebergs off the west coast of the Antarctic Peninsula where the continent was first sighted. Breathtaking escarpments of snow and ice swept down from dark outcroppings of rock to the shores of the freezing sea.

Amundsen was on watch at the helm one night while the expedition was navigating a narrow strait. Uncharted land lurked on both sides. Suddenly Amundsen saw a dark stripe. Realizing it was land, he turned the ship hard in the opposite direction, narrowly averting disaster. Although he wasn't a church-goer, he didn't have any doubts that God was watching over everything. Like other polar explorers, he had a deep belief in Providence.

While the expedition mapped the region, numerous landings were made, during which Amundsen participated in the first skiing, sledging, and camping in Antarctica.

They continued on, crossing the Antarctic Circle six months after leaving Europe. Before them the glistening pack ice stretched to the horizon. Shifting ice floes, often riding up on top of one another, sounded like what an earlier explorer described as "the distant murmur of a city at the bottom of a valley." It was an awesome spectacle.

But the sailors were in much greater danger than they could imagine. It was now late in February, with the austral winter on the way. De Gerlache realized his original plans couldn't succeed. The 31-year-old baron, however, was determined to reach the farthest point south and become the first man to winter in the Antarctic. Risking everyone's life, he ordered the ship on, while giving the sailors the impression they were heading home.

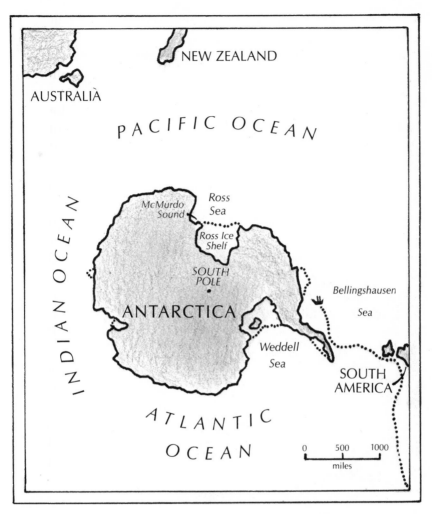

Dotted line marks the route of the Belgica *from South America to its icy incarceration at 71°31′S, 85°16′W.*

Only Amundsen and the second-in-command knew the truth.

By March 2, the crew found themselves one hundred miles within the ice pack, surrounded by ice, all channels closed. They had insufficient food, no warm clothing (except those of the shore party), and not enough lamps to light all the quarters.

Adrien de Gerlache, the leader of the Belgica *Expedition*

They were in serious trouble, and Amundsen was delighted. This kind of ordeal was what he wanted.

For thirteen horrendous months the ship remained fast in the grip of the ice. Around it, the scene never seemed to change. During the winter the men didn't see the sun for several months. Then, following a short twilight period, the sun blazed continuously from a cold, blue sky and there was no darkness. But more than the strange climate and the monotony, the explorers had to suffer one another and the fear they would never escape.

Two of the sailors went insane during the months of waiting. Scurvy swept the ship like a plague. Without any fresh food in their diet to prevent the disease, all were stricken with its symptoms. Amundsen, Dr. Cook, and one other were affected but not disabled, leaving them to care for the rest and to do the chores.

Dr. Cook knew from his Arctic experience that fresh meat could be used to counteract scurvy. So those who were able began to lay in a stock of seals and penguins alongside the ship. The skipper, however, regarded this as a personal criticism of his choice of food. He only allowed the meat to be served on occasion for the few who were willing to try it. One of the officers developed such a mania about eating such flesh that he insisted he would rather die than try it. He died of scurvy on June 5 and was buried without ceremony in a hole in the ice. Afterward, every time the ice groaned eerily against the hull of the ship, the sailors were haunted by the reminder of his body floating beneath them.

De Gerlache and the second-in-command became so ill that they were laid up in bed, leaving Amundsen in charge. Displaying his enterprising character, the Norseman located a carefully hoarded store of red blankets and had them made into loose-fitting suits for the men. He turned out the few men capable of working and uncovered the frozen cache of seals and penguins.

But it was Dr. Cook who saved the expedition. He inspired enough faith in the crew to get them to take as medicine the penguin meat they had refused as food. Within a week everyone's health had improved, at least physically, due to this simple change in diet.

When the sun burst into the bitter skies above the *Belgica* on July 23, the toll taken by the first experience of an Antarctic winter became strikingly evident. Personalities had changed, faces had aged years. Amundsen's hair had turned gray, even though he was only twenty-six. But he and Dr. Cook appeared to be in the best condition, undoubtedly because they had worked hard all winter improving their polar equipment instead of focusing on impending disaster.

Hopes revived with the return of the sun. Dr. Cook led small parties to search for indications of where the ice might even-

Belgica *crewmen haul snow for drinking water.*

tually break open and provide a lead, or channel, for the ship to escape. But throughout the short summer, the ice showed no indication of giving way. Another winter edged toward them. Three sailors were now insane, and Dr. Cook was concerned about the mental health of De Gerlache.

After assessing the situation, Dr. Cook believed the ship could be freed if they could get it into a lead in the ice less than a mile away. When the pack ice began to move, the channel would open up, providing an escape route to the open sea. But this involved cutting a canal through the ice to reach the channel.

The doctor's plan must have sounded like madness to the weak and apathetic crew. But it provided the spark to break their depression. It gave them something to do. On January 11, the work began with four-foot saws and explosives of tonite—a job the men completed after weeks of hard work.

After towing the ship through the canal to the lead, they waited for another tedious month within tantalizing sight of the sea. Finally, the lead widened. Freedom!

As the ship headed toward open water, it was forced to squeeze between two giant icebergs. The beleaguered vessel inched its way between the monoliths for several days. At times the men couldn't hear anything said to them because of the noise of the ice grinding and breaking off against the sides of the ship. Had they endured so much only to be crushed to death at the last moment?

Again, Dr. Cook had a plan. He had carefully preserved the skins of the penguins they had killed earlier, which he was taking home as trophies. He had these made into mats and lowered over the side of the ship to cushion it against the impact of the ice. The penguin-skin bumpers worked, and the ship was saved.

Although the voyage had been arduous, the historic sojourn in the pack ice had enabled the expedition to conduct a longer series of scientific observations in the unexplored Antarctic than had ever been achieved before. It brought back an entire

Dr. Frederick Cook. Although Cook was later discredited as an explorer, Amundsen remained his friend.

year's meteorological record, establishing that a ring of low pressure surrounds the anticyclone area of the continent. On this information the first climatology of the Antarctic was based. The expedition was also notable because it taught a young man named Roald Amundsen the ABC's of polar exploration.

While Amundsen was enduring the sunless Antarctic winter, Ellsworth, then a high-school senior, was marveling at a sunset that stirred his ambitions for the future. He had gone on a camping trip to Yellowstone Park and watched in awe as the sun set on the Continental Divide. He claimed later that the brief trip did more for him than all of the schools and teachers he had known. He had found himself at last, although he didn't quite know it yet. His safe, comfortable, routine existence, he said, was lost forever in the radiance of that western sunset.

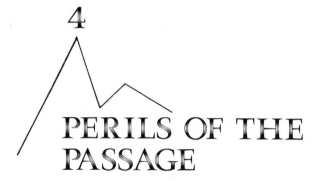

4

PERILS OF THE PASSAGE

Ellsworth's first chance to experience unknown lands came in 1903 when he joined the initial survey party of the Canadian Pacific Railway, exploring and surveying for the first Canadian transcontinental line. Without a second thought, he dropped out of Columbia University in the spring of 1903 just before final exams began. He was hired as an axman on the survey gang in southwest Ontario.

His future mentor, meanwhile, had arrived among the islands

Lauritz Haaland's painting of the Gjøa *in the Northwest Passage*

of the Canadian Arctic, 1700 miles to the north, to begin tackling the Northwest Passage. Unknown to each other, both men were blazing new routes across Canada.

The 31-year-old Amundsen had spent his inheritance to buy a 69-foot sloop, *Gjøa* (Yoo-ah), in hopes of becoming the first to navigate the Northwest Passage. For centuries Europeans had been frustrated in their attempts to discover this shortcut through nine hundred miles of tricky channels between the islands of the Canadian Arctic from Greenland to Alaska. Hundreds of lives had been lost during some sixty attempts. The route was a mariner's nightmare.

Although some of the biggest names in the British Navy had been foiled by the passage, Amundsen believed he would succeed. Instead of trying to crash through the ice in a large vessel, as others had done, Amundsen's strategy was to use a small ship to push his way between the ice floes. The old-timers thought he was mad. The 47-ton *Gjøa* was too small to survive in the ice pack.

To nearly everyone's surprise, the little sloop made it through Baffin Bay and Lancaster Sound, despite freezing fog, gales, and icebergs. At desolate Beechey Island in the heart of the Canadian Arctic, the seven explorers dropped anchor. Above the shingly beach, three forlorn crosses marked the graves of men who had perished there in search of the fabled passage.

The crew erected a declination needle ashore and crouched around watching the oscillations that determined their route to the North Magnetic Pole. Fixing the location of the northern center of the earth's magnetic field was their important scientific mission. This had enabled them to win the necessary backing for the voyage by giving it a "worthwhile" purpose. The magnetic pole had apparently moved since the British explorer James Ross first located it at Cape Adelaide on Boothia Peninsula. Amundsen was determined to find the new position. By doing so, he could prove the theory that the pole shifted, and he could calculate the direction and rate of the pole's movement.

Heading toward Cape Adelaide, the *Gjøa* entered Peel Sound where earlier ships had been stopped by the ice. But instead of ice, a glassy smooth sea greeted the voyagers. They were worried by the lack of movement, however. It suggested that an impenetrable fortress of ice lay ahead.

Amundsen paced the deck anxiously. Then he felt the boards under his feet begin to move. It was a swell under the boat, a message from the open sea. The water to the south was open! It seemed to Amundsen as though Providence had picked his little ship to be the one to succeed.

When the expedition sailed by Cape Adelaide, Amundsen confirmed Ross' positioning of the pole somewhere in the area. But this welcomed position was also perilous. Their magnetic compass, which they desperately needed because of thick fog surrounding them, was useless in the vicinity of the pole. Amundsen was forced to risk everything by steering a course

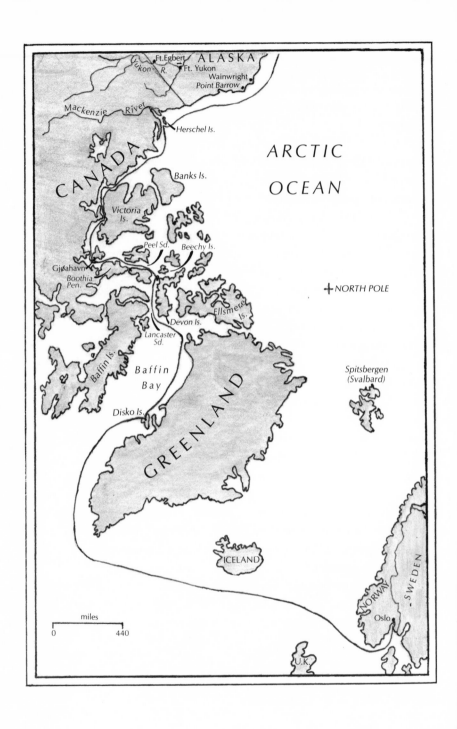

Ft.Egbert ALASKA
Ft. Yukon
Yukon R.
Wainwright
Point Barrow

Mackenzie River
Herschel Is.

ARCTIC

CANADA

OCEAN

Banks Is.

Victoria
Is.

Peel Sd.
Beechy Is.

Gjøahavn
Boothia
Pen.

NORTH POLE

Ellsmere
Is.

Devon Is.

Lancaster
Sd.

Spitsbergen
(Svalbard)

Baffin Is.

Baffin
Bay

Disko Is.

GREENLAND

ICELAND

NORWAY

SWEDEN

Oslo

miles

0   440

U.K.

according to what seemed to be the wind direction. Every man stood nerve-straining, six-hour watches on deck each night because of the danger. Seventeen fierce Eskimo dogs, straining at their tethers to tear into one another, didn't make the job any easier.

They struck the submerged tip of one island but escaped without serious damage. Then the engineer, Peder Ristvedt, reported that one of the fuel tanks was leaking. Although the leak wasn't serious, it had to be stopped or the little engine room, packed tightly with fuel tanks, would become saturated with kerosene and its fumes. Amundsen directed him to pump the contents of the leaking tank into a safe container.

That evening before retiring the captain was recording the day's activities when he heard someone shout, "Fire!" He rushed up on deck to see flames shooting up through the skylight of the engine room. Calling out instructions, he joined the men, scooping up buckets of sea water to douse the blaze.

After the flames had been stifled, the crew realized how dangerous the fire had been. Before the leaking fuel tank had been emptied that morning, cleaning materials left in the compartment had been soaked. The seven explorers narrowly had escaped being scattered over the Canadian Arctic.

Their troubles, however, were just beginning. James Ross Strait, in which they were sailing, was uncharted. They had to "feel" their way along by making soundings with a lead-weighted line. At one point, Amundsen had the helm and Anton Lund was heaving the lead. Eight fathoms, then nine fathoms, the first mate called out—plenty of water beneath the keel. The weather seemed to be cooperating, too.

Ristvedt came out on deck and began hoisting the sails. Abandoning his watch momentarily, Lund went to help the engineer. Suddenly the men heard the sickening sound of the ship

LEFT: *Line indicates the Northwest Passage as navigated by the* Gjøa.

grounding on the rocks of a shoal reef. Just as abruptly, the *Gjøa* floated free.

The captain put the ship hard to starboard to avoid the danger, but the vessel grounded once more. Again it slipped free, then shuddered to a halt. Scrambling up the mast, Amundsen discovered the *Gjøa* was hung up on a large reef. He ordered a few of the men to lower one of the small boats and take soundings. They found that the best course lay straight ahead, even though two hundred yards of reef had to be crossed in that direction and the water depth in places was only six feet—too shallow for the eight-foot draft of the *Gjøa*.

Jettison the cases of pemmican! Amundsen ordered. The ship had to be lightened, even though the dried rations were their primary source of food. Struggling with the 100-pound cases, the crew pushed twenty-five of them over the side. Then they shifted the remaining deck cargo to make the ship heel over and raise its keel. Hopefully, when the high tide came, the ship would be lifted over the obstacle and into deep water. But the high tide came and left with the *Gjøa* still stuck. Two hours later, the crew turned in, leaving the skipper alone on watch.

Early in the morning, Amundsen roused the men. "The wind is freshening," he told them, "and it's in the direction we want to go. If it develops into a storm, let's try blowing ourselves off this rock."

All hands turned to and raised the sails as a gale started to howl. Scraping and splintering, the ship lurched over the obstacle. As it neared the end of the reef, Amundsen could see patches of foaming water where rocks protruded through the surface.

Abandon ship! he ordered, fearing the *Gjøa* would break up.

Before the small boats were lowered, Lund suggested they try throwing the remaining deck cargo overboard. Amundsen agreed. Working in freezing sea spray and sleet, they maneuvered the heavy crates into the churning sea. Next, the hold was opened and the boxes stacked at the top were heaved over the side.

Lightened, the *Gjøa* pounded along faster across the reef. Several times the vessel was lifted by the sea and brought crashing down on the rocks. Amundsen raced up to the crow's nest to navigate for Godfred Hansen, who took over at the helm.

With a shudder the ship slid off the reef, leaving a wake of splinters behind. But then the ship wouldn't steer. A quick investigation revealed the *Gjøa* hadn't escaped unscathed from the shoals as believed. The metal pins that held the rudder in place had been nearly knocked out of position. If the rudder was pushed backward or to the side, the pins might fall out, leaving the ship rudderless in the unexplored Arctic. Then, miraculously, the ship was jarred again and the pins dropped back into place!

The drenched and exhausted crew sailed on, barely to escape once again from a violent gale. This one nearly drove them ashore at Boothia Peninsula. But the greater danger was the rapidly approaching winter. They had to find a safe haven to berth the ship before it set in.

As if on cue, a mile-long cove, which they named Gjøahavn, appeared on the south coast of King William Island. It was sheltered by low hills and situated only ninety miles from the North Magnetic Pole, making it an ideal position for their scientific work. Special wooden observatories, a storehouse, a hut for

James Ross, British explorer and rear admiral, in 1831 became the first to locate the North Magnetic Pole. Ten years later, in Antarctica, Ross discovered the Ross Ice Shelf, including the Bay of Whales.

explosives, a firehouse, and kennels for the dogs were erected ashore.

As part of their winter routine, the men skiied to stay in shape and hunted caribou, which gave them fresh food and a safeguard against scurvy. Amundsen didn't take part in the killing, choosing to transport the carcasses to the ship. He was a poor shot and didn't enjoy hunting because he had been appalled by the slaughter of seals while serving on Arctic sealing ships.

The voyagers soon found something else living on King William Island. Eskimo. Armed with bows and arrows, a small band appeared on the skyline one October day and began advancing downhill toward the tiny settlement. Amundsen felt uneasy. He pictured his little party as easy prey for plunder.

Caribou, shown here grazing in summer, provided fresh food as

The young leader and two of his men grabbed their rifles and went to meet the Netsiliks. At about fifteen yards the two groups stopped, eyeing one another. As the tension mounted, Amundsen told his men to make a big show of throwing down their rifles. Imitating the move, the Eskimo leader uttered a command to his followers, who also threw down their weapons. Amundsen, unarmed, advanced toward the Eskimo as their leader came forward to meet him. Amundsen knew his gestures, expressions, and tone of voice would be carefully interpreted by the natives.

"Teima!" Amundsen shouted, remembering the word he had been told meant a hearty hello.

The Eskimo leader hesitated momentarily, then replied in kind: *"Minaktumi!"*

well as clothing in the Arctic.

Running toward them, the hunting party embraced the *kabluna* (white men) and patted them with their hands. These Eskimo had never seen *kabluna* before, but their grandfathers had encountered James Ross during his search for the North Magnetic Pole. The story of that meeting with the godlike white men had been told and retold so that the Eskimo knew it well.

The Norsemen led the Eskimo to the *Gjøa* and gave them caribou to eat. Later, Amundsen accompanied the natives to their camp. When they arrived, the Eskimo rushed ahead, shouting, *"Kabluna! Kabluna!"* Inhabitants poured out of a half-dozen igloos. Standing in the dim light falling from the igloo windows, they stared, shouted to one another, plucked at the white man's clothing, and patted him to determine his makeup.

Amundsen was taken to a banquet of raw caribou in one of the large igloos. As was customary, none of the village women were present. The men sat around hacking off pieces of raw meat, which they ate with great gusto.

When the meal was over, the village women were allowed to enter and examine the tall *kabluna* with the piercing blue eyes. At first they visually inspected him. Becoming bolder, they began to feel his clothes and then to stroke and pat him. They missed nothing, Amundsen said, and when they departed, they knew all there was to know about his body.

To sleep, the Norwegian was escorted to a large igloo occupied by two families who proceeded to strip before crawling in between hides of fur. The igloo, heated by an open lamp with a wick of twisted moss, was hot, stinking, and smoky. The families crowded together to make room for the guest in their beds, but Amundsen opted for unrolling his sleeping bag on the floor between them.

Amundsen had plenty of opportunity to observe the North American Eskimo during the first winter that the *Gjøa* lay frozen in the ice at King William Island. When he invited them to visit, they arrived with their families, dogs, and all of their pos-

Nechilli Eskimo in their igloo

sessions. They built igloos and set up camp.

Each evening between seven and nine o'clock, open house was held on the ship and the natives clamored aboard to gawk at such wonders as tin pans and pencils. Grunting in amazement, they observed the *kabluna* as they went about their daily life. Because the Eskimo reeked and were often infected with lice, the crew weren't anxious for them to linger long aboard the ship. The explorers soon found that by turning up the stove the heat encouraged the departure of their guests, who were dressed in bulky caribou-skin clothing and sealskin boots.

Before long the Scandinavians appeared to have gone native. They discarded their wool clothes for the lightweight Eskimo furs that, because of a loose fit, kept them warm without sweating. They learned to build igloos and to handle the Eskimo dogs. Helmer Hanssen became an expert in understanding the unique personality of the Eskimo breed and how to relate to the wolf-like animal. The Eskimo husky could be a bully, thief, and fighter but was also brave, intelligent, and persevering. Hanssen found the dogs to be hard-working social animals, accepting a leader but ready to chew him up if given the chance to replace him.

While Amundsen lived among the Eskimo, Ellsworth, farther south, was working with Ojibway Indians on the railroad's surveying gang. By the time his job as axman had finished in the spring of 1904, Lincoln had changed from "a callow college youth into a bronzed and toughened man of the open." He, too, was preparing for the future.

As wild fowl began to appear that same spring at King William Island, the sun worked to lift the heavy winter mantle from the barren hills and frozen harbor. On March 16, Amundsen set out with Hanssen for the magnetic pole. On the way they met a hunting party of Eskimo, who invited them to visit their village. Amundsen eagerly accepted.

Whooping with delight, the Eskimo hitched their dog teams with the Norwegians' for a grand procession to the village. The huskies, however, were less enthusiastic and fights broke out as the group went along. But this didn't worry the Eskimo. Laughing and shouting, they would rush in among the vicious dogs and force them apart as though it were a game they all enjoyed.

View of the Gjøa frozen in for its long stay at Gjøahavn

The parade eventually reached the village, halting near the compound of sixteen igloos. Looking fat and greasy, with dirt-caked hands and faces, the women of the tribe emerged in a single file to greet them. To the guests' relief, the women did their inspecting from a distance.

The two Norsemen built a large igloo for the night so they wouldn't risk catching any parasites that might be carried by the Eskimo's fur clothes. Amundsen also wanted to display his knowledge of igloo-building. While they worked on the project, the Eskimo gathered around, commenting and laughing loudly. Amundsen soon found he wasn't as adept at snow-hut construction as he had thought. He was forced to ask his giggling hosts for help.

The next day, the Eskimo presented their guests with gifts of lovely fur garments. Amundsen was thankful, but disappointed. He wanted fur underwear. Taking aside Atikleura, son of the medicine man and one of the cleanest-looking men of the tribe, he inquired about a swap. When Atikleura finally understood what Amundsen wanted, he accepted the request as an honor.

An Ogluli Eskimo, one of those studied by Roald Amundsen, repairs a sledge.

He took his guest inside the igloo and began stripping, while Amundsen tried in vain to stop him. Atikleura's wife looked on approvingly as the proud Eskimo handed his underwear to the *kabluna* and insisted he put it on. To avoid offending him, Amundsen accepted the gift and, despite the likelihood of lice, took a fur from the bed and modestly wrapped up in it to change.

Amundsen and Hanssen eventually traveled far enough to establish a food depot for use on a second journey and returned to Gjøahavn. Other members of the expedition had been out sledging in the opposite direction.

On April 6, Amundsen decided to make another try for the pole. He set out with Ristvedt and they were quickly schooled in the difficulties of polar travel overland: soft wet snow, rough sea ice, fog, blistering winds, and glaring sun. Ten days later, they reached the spot on Boothia Peninsula where Ross had fixed the pole's location. Determining that the pole had moved northward, Amundsen became the first to prove the theory of magnetic pole migration.

The two explorers chased the fluctuations of the pole around Boothia Peninsula for the next three weeks, during which time they lost two dogs when they were attacked by a hungry polar bear. Because of blowing snow, they were unable to pin down the pole's exact location and, unaware, may have passed over it. Amundsen decided to head back, even though he couldn't claim to have stood exactly at the pole. It is said to be one of the few goals he never achieved, but in fact he probably did become the first to reach the North Magnetic Pole.

Perhaps of greater importance were the surveying and charting journeys that the explorers made over what was one of the last unknown stretches of North America.

A year later, in June, open water appeared beyond the tiny harbor, much earlier than the preceding year. Hopes for escape ran high. Nineteen months of magnetic observations stopped.

The ship was readied. The weeks passed. The men agonized. Would they be forced to spend a third winter in that awful place?

Two months dragged by before the northeast winds broke up the ice and the *Gjøa* sailed out of its haven. The explorers took with them a seventeen-year-old Eskimo, Manni, who had begged and pleaded to go until he persuaded Amundsen. Manni was anxious to learn to read and write and wanted to become a part of the *kabluna*'s world. But he was never to see that world.

Searching for a water route among the islands, Amundsen and his men headed toward Alaska. (Ellsworth, by coincidence, was then working in Alaska. He had taken a job in a gold-mine development fifty miles from Teller, a town that would become a landmark in the Amundsen-Ellsworth partnership twenty-one years later.)

For four days the Norsemen picked their way through more hazardous, uncharted waters. Because of his constant vigilance and fear of failure, Amundsen couldn't sleep or eat. He looked tired and much older than his thirty-three years. But his tiny ship managed to reach the entrance to the straits between Victoria Island and the mainland. Although not home safe yet, he knew he had won the battle. The passage had been navigated previously to that point from the west. He, an unknown explorer from a small nation, had solved the link that had frustrated so many!

A week later, Lieutenant Hansen burst into his cabin. "Ship in sight, sir!"

Amundsen said nothing. But as the realization struck, the impassive explorer began to feel a "strangeness" in his throat and in his eyes. Hurrying topside, he joined his jubilant companions gawking at the topsails of an American whaler heeling before the wind.

Suddenly he felt hungry. Grabbing a knife, he rushed up the rigging where caribou carcasses were hanging. He furiously hacked off chunks of raw, half-frozen meat, wolfing them down

The Eskimo boy Manni

like a famished animal. Although his stomach rejected this bar-
barous feast, he tried again. This time he was able to keep the
food down.

Amundsen and his men expected the rest of the voyage to be
a pleasure trip, but a week later they found themselves locked

A view of the Yukon at about the time Amundsen traveled it with Captain Mogg

in the ice off King Point in Mackenzie Bay, near the Alaskan border. It was their third winter in the Arctic. Happily, this time they had some fellow mariners for company. Stuck in the ice nearby were six American whaling ships, which were under orders from their companies to provide all possible assistance to the *Gjøa*.

Amundsen was anxious to be the one to announce his historic news, for which certain newspapers had paid to obtain the exclusive rights. But he had no money.

Luckily, one of the whaling captains, William Mogg, planned to make an overland journey to civilization where he could make arrangements for another ship. Since he had no sledging experience, the old salt took Amundsen and two Eskimo guides with him.

Amundsen and the Eskimo ran beside the sledges while the portly Mogg rode in all his plump splendor. The sixty-year-old seafarer was in no condition to do otherwise.

They set off to reach the nearest telegraph office, five hundred miles south across mountains, forests, and deep snow. The journey was the first test of the cold-weather techniques Amundsen had learned from the Eskimo, techniques that would later enable him to win his most famous victory. It was also a testimonial to his remarkable physical condition, determination, and love of cold climates. No doubt the challenge appealed to him, too.

Although they got bogged down repeatedly in heavy snow, the party covered twenty-five to thirty miles a day. But the meager rations of beans, which Mogg had insisted on taking for food, proved to be inadequate—for everyone except Mogg. The three runners were soon dangerously thin and hungry.

Despite their condition, Mogg insisted they not waste time by halting for lunch. When Amundsen protested, the captain reminded him who was the boss.

Amundsen remained silent until the next day. Halfway between roadhouses, he stopped the huskies and told Mogg to

Amundsen in Alaska following the navigation of the Northwest Passage

take the team and go on alone through the wilderness.

Mogg was nearly frightened to death. He pleaded with Amundsen not to leave him and quickly agreed to the Norwegian's demands for three meals a day.

The party reached Fort Egbert, now Eagle City, in forty-two days. Amundsen fired off the news of his victory to Europe, but the dispatch was intercepted by a major in the United States Signal Corps in Seattle and leaked to the local press.

Amundsen waited at the fort for two months until letters arrived for his crew. Then he started the grueling, five-week trek back. At least this time he didn't have Captain Mogg along.

Soon after the leader's return to the *Gjøa*, the engineer, Gustav Wiik, died of appendicitis. There was no doctor aboard because Amundsen believed a doctor would be a drawback on any expedition. He thought a medical man would refuse to do anything outside of his field of work. Amundsen needed versatile men. So he settled for one who had first-aid training. Except in the case of the unfortunate Wiik, the gamble always paid off, though it indicated the risks Amundsen was willing to take.

While the voyagers waited through that summer of 1906 for the ice to break up, the young Eskimo, Manni, was lost. He took a small boat to shoot ducks one day, fell overboard, and disappeared before help could reach him. Like most Eskimo of the region, he didn't know how to swim.

The expedition finally got away on August 10. As if Nature didn't want it to be too easy for them, ice bent the propeller shaft, and the gaff supporting the sail snapped. The *Gjøa* limped around Alaska's Cape Prince of Wales on August 30. There, after so long a time battling narrow channels, lay the great expanse of the Pacific Ocean. The explorers had navigated 3450 miles of deadly Arctic waters since leaving the west coast of Greenland.

In the fading twilight of the next day they saw the twinkling lights of Nome. Suddenly a giant searchlight picked them out of the darkness. All kinds of boats, virtually anything that would float, quickly surrounded them.

Gjøa *arrives in Nome after three years in the Arctic.*

The Gjøa *crew in Nome, Alaska: (front row, left to right) Amundsen, Peder Ristvedt, Adolf Lindstrøm, Helmer Hanssen; (top row, left to right) Godfred Hansen, Anton Lund, and two unidentified volunteers*

By C.L. Andrews

Capt. Amundsen sloop "Gjøa"

Amundsen photographed after the voyage of the Gjøa

That most enthusiastic of Amundsen's admirers, Lincoln Ellsworth, at the time was chief engineer in charge of laying out the site for Prince Rupert, Canada. The future town was to be the Pacific terminal of the Grand Pacific Railway, several lines of which Ellsworth had helped to survey. In five years he had changed from a discontented college boy, unable to pass an examination in any subject, into a civil engineer holding a responsible post with a great railroad. He was on his way to discovering his career as an explorer. During the ensuing years he would always find himself "homesick for frontiers," and seeking hardship and adventure in "wild and little-trodden regions."

A LITTLE DETOUR

NORTH POLE REACHED! Newspapers around the world headlined the momentous news on September 1, 1909. Amundsen's friend Dr. Cook alleged to have gained the pole by sledging across the ice floes. Then a week later the papers carried the startling claim by Commander Robert Peary that he, too, had made it to the pole.

Home in New York City, Lincoln Ellsworth was fascinated and closely followed the ensuing dispute. If only he could have been on such an adventure!

To Amundsen it didn't matter who won the controversy. For two years he had been organizing his own expedition to capture the pole. It was part of his plan to prove Fridtjof Nansen's theory that a ship could drift across the Arctic while caught up in the ice.

Reporters were soon telephoning for his reactions. Would his plans be affected? Amundsen was careful not to pass judgment, but he was definite that his intentions wouldn't change. There was enough scientific value in his expedition to continue.

Dr. Cook, meanwhile, urged Amundsen to change his mind. Shoot for the South Pole, Dr. Cook argued. There was nothing to be gained by repeating a journey to the North Pole. Amundsen decided his former shipmate from the *Belgica* was right, although it meant a radical revision of his plans.

Because of the direction in which the Arctic ice moves, Amundsen had intended to enter the ice pack north of Alaska, which involved sailing around South America to get there. Why not make "a little detour" to the South Pole while passing by Antarctica? Few explorers would have entertained such an am-

In his study, Amundsen prepares for the South Pole expedition.

Hjalmar Johansen

bitious and daring idea, but Amundsen was exceptional.

Only a few days after this decision, Captain Robert Scott of the British Navy announced his second scientific expedition to the Antarctic, during which he hoped to reach the South Pole. News of the British competitor heightened the need for secrecy about Amundsen's new goal. Since Norway depended on Britain's support for its newly won independence, Amundsen feared the Norwegian Government and his supporters would try to stop him if they knew of his plans. They would fear antagonizing what was then the world's greatest power.

Pretending to be continuing preparations for his Polar Basin Drift Expedition, Amundsen worked to bring together the most professional polar expedition ever mounted using dog sledge and ski. Unlike Scott, Amundsen didn't organize from a desk. He used his polar experience, innovative genius, and foresight to improve or design new equipment. He chose hardy companions who were experts in skiing and in dog driving. In today's parlance, he wanted a highly trained squad of commandos for what was going to be a raid on the South Pole.

There was one flaw. Amundsen was compelled by his principal supporter, Nansen, to accept Hjalmar Johansen on the team. Johansen, who had saved Nansen's life during their famous Arctic expedition, was older, equally experienced, and a better skier than Amundsen. He represented a threat to Amundsen's leadership. He was also a potential disaster for any polar expedition. Unemployed, bankrupt, and separated from his family, he had become a heavy drinker.

Only the ship's officers knew of the planned detour when the *Fram* sailed from Amundsen's backyard fjord at midnight on August 9, 1910. Others, however, were already suspicious. On board were ninety-seven Greenland huskies. Why were these animals being carried around the world to Alaska when dogs could be picked up there?

The "Chief," as Amundsen's men called him, dropped the bombshell when the *Fram* docked at Funchal in the Madeira Islands for fresh supplies. He outlined his scheme and asked each man individually if he were willing to stay on. Everyone voted to go, although several admitted afterward they would have refused if others had also objected.

Leon was assigned the responsibility of taking letters from the men to their relatives and announcing the "extension" of his brother's expedition. Leon was also given a telegram for Scott, who had left England some months previously: "Beg leave to inform you proceeding Antarctic—Amundsen." Scott received it on October 12 during a stopover in Melbourne, Australia.

The British press immediately cried foul play, but Scott refused to face the possibility of being upstaged and forged ahead as planned. Amundsen never dismissed the competition. During the four months it took the *Fram* to reach Antarctica, he seemed obsessed with perfecting his equipment. Special care was given to the huskies because success depended on them.

Some of the dogs were so vicious in the beginning that food had to be thrown to them at mealtimes. When the handlers and the dogs got to know one another, the dogs were muzzled and let loose to get all the fight out of their system. Later, Amundsen removed the muzzles and allowed the huskies to run free, which

Skua gulls feed on slaughtered Weddell seals at the Bay of Whales. The Fram *is in the background.*

hitherto had been unthinkable. It was a wise move. Life on board soon revolved around the dogs. They provided an opportunity for diversion and a safety valve for pent up frustrations.

Without making any additional ports of call, the *Fram* continued south. This voyage of sixteen thousand miles in a vessel only 119 feet in length was in itself a remarkable feat.

A gleaming 200-foot wall of ice loomed up before the Norwegians on January 12. They had reached their destination, the Ross Ice Shelf, then called the Great Barrier. Covering an area nearly the size of Texas, this shelf is a massive floating tongue of ice formed by glaciers pouring down from mountains in the interior. Frequently, the cliff-like edge of the Barrier breaks off, forming giant flat-topped icebergs that ocean currents carry north until they break up and melt.

At an inlet the British explorer Ernest Shackleton called the Bay of Whales, Amundsen anchored his ship. Spotted Weddell seals, basking in the intense sun, ignored the intruders, and raucous Adélie penguins streamed across the sea ice to inspect the visitors.

Amundsen carefully studied the ice shelf and decided it wasn't as precarious as his precursors feared. Some places appeared to be stable. By establishing his base on one of these spots, he would be sixty-nine miles closer to the South Pole than Scott's site at McMurdo Sound.

As it turned out, Amundsen's gamble was a greater risk than anyone realized for a long time. The area of the ice shelf where his expedition built its winter quarters was floating, not grounded. Some of the buildings of Little America III, the base built there by the American explorer Richard Byrd in 1940, were seen in the face of an iceberg floating north in 1963.

Ten days after their arrival, the Norwegians had established their station, Framheim, on the ice shelf. It was Spartan, providing 26' x 13' living quarters. Only a table, four double bunks, and a stool for each man furnished the interior.

Framheim, Amundsen's shore base

Scott's ship, the Terra Nova, *arrives at the Bay of Whales.*

Some members of the shore party began laying in a stock of penguins and seals, which cooperated by coming up to inspect the ship where they could be killed easily. For some of the men this was too easy. They went hunting and shot a few seals for sport, leaving them behind on the ice. When Amundsen found out, he was furious. He forbade his men to kill any animals that couldn't be used and made them retrieve the carcasses. Oscar Wisting later remarked that he had never met a man with such a love for animals as Amundsen, contrary to his ruthless image.

On February 4, the *Fram*'s watchman was startled to see Scott's ship, the *Terra Nova,* sail into the bay. Not knowing the British attitude, he dashed for a gun and an English grammar book. He looked up "How are you this morning?" Then concealing the book and the weapon under his coat, he braced himself for the unannounced rivals.

Scott wasn't aboard the *Terra Nova*. He was thirty-five miles across the Barrier in the process of laying a string of supply depots to be used on the trek to the pole during the following summer.

The encounter at the Bay of Whales turned out to be polite and friendly. Three of the British officers were invited to Framheim for breakfast. In a reciprocal gesture, Amundsen and two others were invited to lunch on the *Terra Nova*. Amundsen flabbergasted his competitors by racing his dog team right up to the ship and with a whistle stopping them all at once. He then turned the empty sledge over and left the huskies in their traces, where they remained without fighting until he returned.

Scott had brought thirty-two dogs with him, but only as support for his primary transport—Manchurian ponies brought from Asia and tractor-like motor sledges. He was prejudiced against sledge dogs because he didn't know much about them and on his first Antarctic expedition they had performed miserably.

Although both sides carefully guarded their tactics during the Bay of Whales visit, Amundsen was misled to believe that one of Scott's motor sledges had already crossed the ice shelf.

Six days later, Amundsen set off with three of the seven-man shore party to establish the first of the Norwegian supply depots across the Barrier. Unlike Scott's route, this segment had never been traveled before.

With Kristian Prestrud, a champion skier, striding ahead of the dogs to encourage them on, the four sped over the ice shelf, planting bamboo poles with black flags to mark the route. The pole-seekers eventually cached three tons of provisions across the ice shelf: nearly two tons at 80° S, 100 miles south; half a ton at 81° S, 160 miles south; and half a ton at 82° S, 230 miles south. Most of the food was pemmican, usually a mixture of meat and fat used by explorers before the advent of dehydrated

The Norwegian shore party works on altering clothing after dinner: (left to right) Olav Bjaaland, Sverre Hassel, Oscar Wisting, Helmer Hanssen, Roald Amundsen, Hjalmar Johansen, Kristian Prestrud, and Jørgen Stubberud. Photo was taken by the cook, Adolf Lindstrøm.

food. Amundsen had formulated his own brand by adding oatmeal and peas to help improve digestion. Typical pemmican often caused constipation or diarrhea—serious problems on a polar trek.

Always looking for aspects that needed improving, Amundsen decided the customary black flag on top of each depot was inadequate to mark the cache in the featureless landscape. He had pennants staked in the snow for miles on either side on each supply site. Snow beacons were also built along the route.

As the winter darkness moved in on the two rival outposts on the lonely continent, Amundsen and his companions considered every way to reduce the weight of their equipment and increase their speed.

Amundsen ruled by the force of his personality, but he was

63

Amundsen's breath freezes in the cold air.

creative and sensitive to the strains of confinement. He organized a contest to guess the temperature in order to get the men out into the fresh air every morning to rid themselves of "morning peevishness." There was also a dart competition, and holiday celebrations to break up the weekly routine, as is the case at Antarctic stations today. On Saturday nights the men enjoyed a ritual sauna, finished off by a naked dash through the icy tunnel to the hut.

Feeding the dogs, which were allowed to roam freely, was another diversion. On one occasion, Amundsen wrestled in the snow with a dog called Shark, forcing open the husky's jaws to release a piece of meat stolen from another dog. Whatever he did, Amundsen projected self-confidence, but he was deeply worried about the British motor sledges. After all his careful planning, would he be beaten by a machine?

The sun appeared on August 24, heightening the men's anticipation as they waited anxiously for the temperature to rise. One day it was so cold that, instead of ice forming in the nostril hair as it usually did, Amundsen's entire nose froze.

They made a start for the pole on September 8, but it was too early in the season. Temperatures plummeted to as low as −69° F. The men's breath froze in the air and they were miserable in the tent that night. The fluid in their compass froze and two dogs froze when they lay down. The party was forced to return after reaching the first depot.

During the homeward journey, Amundsen, Wisting, and Hanssen raced on ahead, arriving hours before the others. The last to get back were Johansen and Prestrud. They had been delayed by their faltering dogs, which had been barely able to pull the empty sledge. Both men were frostbitten. It had been a narrow escape, and Johansen bitterly criticized Amundsen's leadership.

Although Amundsen had made a mistake in not keeping his men together, Johansen had challenged his authority. It was mutiny. Amundsen realized he couldn't risk taking Johansen to the pole. So he decided to send him, with Prestrud and Jørgen Stubberud, to explore King Edward VII Land. Johansen refused, demanding a written order, which Amundsen gave him. Johansen eventually bowed to authority, but Amundsen never forgave his disloyalty, refusing even to speak to him.

Amundsen made a second start for the pole on October 20. He took four men with him, leaving only Lindstrøm, the cook, behind to hold the fort. Dressed in furs, the polar party looked like an Eskimo migration as they headed out across the ice shelf. Since most of the supplies had been depoted, the four sledges were lightly loaded and the men rode most of the way to the southern boundary of the Barrier, about 340 miles.

On their third day out, the men strayed from the flagged route due to poor light and snow blowing in their faces. Suddenly Olav Bjaaland's sledge tipped over and began to disappear. Shouting for help, he jumped free and braced his feet in the snow. The dogs, feeling themselves being drawn into the hole, flattened themselves and dug their claws into the frozen surface. Just as the sledge's traces were tearing apart, the other men arrived with ropes and rescued the lead dogs from the pit.

SOUTH POLE

Last Depot · Shackleton's Farthest South

POLAR

PLATEAU

Devil's Glacier Depot

Butcher's Shop

Axel Heiberg Glacier

Beardmore Glacier

85.5°S Depot

84°S Depot

83°S Depot

82°S Depot

81°S Depot

King Edward VII Land

80°S Depot

SCOTT'S ROUTE

Cape Evans

McMurdo Sound

miles

0   140

LEFT: *Amundsen's and Scott's routes across Antarctica to the South Pole*

The sledge, however, continued to hang over the abyss. Somebody had to be lowered on a rope to remove the cases before the sledge could be brought up. When Amundsen called for a volunteer, everybody wanted the dangerous job. Each was eager to see what the inside of a crevasse looked like. The leader gave Wisting the honor and down he went.

As he dangled in space, the former naval gunner called out a description of what he could see: a deep glistening chasm with its sharp pinnacles of ice. He then informed his colleagues that they were standing on ice only a few inches thick! When he was hauled up, Wisting added that none of them would have escaped if they had gone a few feet farther east. Only a paper-thin crust served as the surface there. Below this lay great spikes of ice on which they would have been impaled.

Securing their tent with guy wires, the Norwegian party prepares camp at the Axel Heiberg Glacier.

After discovering a snow-covered mountain range in the distance,

The polar party couldn't press on until the visibility improved, which forced the men to set up camp with the tent's guy wires stretched across crevasses in every direction. Wisting almost got a second look inside a crevasse when he sank up to his armpits in one while walking from the tent to his sledge. Only his outstretched arms saved him.

Beyond their 81° S cache, the Norsemen found themselves off course once again in a nasty crevasse field. The cracks appeared narrow, however, so Amundsen decided not to stop. Fourteen miles on, Hanssen tripped on his team's traces and fell in the middle of a crevasse, his outstretched body held by a bridge of snow across the pit. His dogs, safely on the far side, seized the opportunity to enjoy a good fight. While Amundsen handled the dogs, Wisting rescued Hanssen—all in a day's work.

The British expedition had finally got underway on November 2. The ponies managed to pull only 450 pounds each as the

the Norwegians stopped at 84° S and built their fifth supply depot.

poor beasts struggled across the Barrier with their handlers marching beside them.

The Norwegians gained their 82° S supply cache and hurried on to 83° S where, on November 9, they built a depot. Two days later, the Chief made his first major discovery: a mountain range like pyramids glittering on the horizon, which he named the Queen Maud Mountains. Like a gauntlet thrown across their path, the rugged, snow-covered peaks loomed closer every day as the explorers pushed on.

They discovered a mighty glacier on the following day. Like a frozen moat, miles in width and breathtakingly steep, the ominous river of ice transected their course. Amundsen named it for Axel Heiberg, patron of the *Gjøa* and *Fram* expeditions.

Day after day, there was exhausting relay work as the men pushed and strained to get the teams up the "road." They looked back at one point and were astounded by what they had

A view of an Antarctic crevasse field

After staking out the dogs in a semicircle, the Norwegian party camps for the day.

come through: "Chasm after chasm, crevasse after crevasse, with great blocks of ice scattered promiscuously about, gave one the impression that here Nature was at her mightiest. . . ." Unknown to them, Amundsen had picked the worst route in the region.

November 21 was the most arduous of the haul, as they crossed wave after wave of rock-hard hummocks. They climbed 5000 feet to an altitude of 10,920 feet before halting. What the dogs had accomplished was a "sheer marvel," Amundsen wrote.

What should have been a time of rejoicing, however, became the saddest moment of the expedition. Twenty-four of the forty-two dogs weren't needed any longer. They were put down as planned earlier. When the drivers armed themselves, Amundsen went inside the tent and pumped up the primus stove, hoping to produce enough noise so he wouldn't hear the shots. In a pot he began preparing the pemmican, stirring it with all of his energy. Then came the first report, and the man of extraordinary courage gave a start. The ensuing rounds made a "gruesome" sound as they cracked the silence over the virgin white plain. An oppressive, miserable feeling enveloped the explorers who had grown so fond of their "faithful servants."

The eighteen remaining huskies were given meat from the butchered dogs, improving their condition. But it was the next day before the men could make themselves eat the cutlets. Although the scene at what became known as Butcher's Shop wasn't easily forgotten, the Norwegians believed the animals had to be sacrificed to attain their goal. The dogs had been treated well and were put down swiftly.

Amundsen's dogs suffered far less than Scott's ponies, which were floundering through deep snow on the ice shelf. The British, as a result, were far behind in the race. Their ponies would eventually be shot before they started through the mountains and the meat used to feed the men and the supporting dog teams. Although the dogs were performing surprisingly well, Scott continued to discount their worth.

To help protect their ponies, snow walls were thrown up by Scott's party at every British camp.

Gale-force winds, driving the crystalized surface snow across the plateau like a blizzard, kept the Norwegians tent bound at Butcher's Shop for two days longer than they intended. The delay, however, was a blessing in disguise. It gave both the men and dogs time to acclimatize to the high altitude, which wasn't fully appreciated at the time.

On their fifth day at the camp, Amundsen decided to push on even though the blizzard continued to rage. They set off joking in the face of adversity. Falling snow mixed with drift, whipping over ripples of hard ice called sastrugi, made it difficult to keep their eyes open. The weather, which had been nearly perfect during the climb through the mountains, had turned against them.

On November 26, they stopped to erect a depot at 86° S. During moments of visibility, they had glimpsed mountain peaks thrusting through the mile-high ice. But ahead the plateau was featureless, and they began building snow beacons as they had on the ice shelf to avoid becoming lost.

What appeared to be a huge glacier, rife with small crevasses, cut across their path on the twenty-ninth. Amundsen proclaimed it Devil's Glacier, although the area actually was a disturbance in the ice cap, much like rapids in a river. But the explorers managed to find an unbroken patch at 86°21′ S, laid another cache and built a six-foot beacon.

For three days they picked their way across Devil's Glacier, their lives at stake with each step. At times they had to scale ice ridges as high as one hundred feet. Gale-strength blizzards that increased the incidence of frostbite made it nearly impossible to see where they were going. The crystalized surface was more like sand then snow, increasing the resistence to their sledges.

On December 4, they traversed an area that looked like a frozen lake, but it turned out to be a thin layer of ice covering a field of crevasses. Here, at what they called the Devil's Ballroom, they had plenty of opportunity to satisfy their curiosity about crevasses.

One runner of Wisting's sledge broke through into a gaping crack. While the dogs clawed for their lives, Bjaaland took a quick photo before rushing to help with the rescue. Soon after, the same team plunged in another hole, hanging by their harness until they were hauled up. Then, it was Bjaaland's turn. He fell in and hit a crust a short distance below the surface. As he was about to crash through this bridge, he barely managed to grip a rope from the sledge and save himself. Amundsen commented that the surface seemed so hollow that it sounded as though they were walking on the tops of empty barrels.

Amundsen and his party cross Devil's Glacier.

Amundsen's party camped on the way to the pole

At 87° S the men finally reached the Polar Plateau after battling for days across the tortured area at the top of the Axel Heiberg Glacier. They expected a smooth run to the pole, but the Antarctic had plenty of surprises—ice ridges, fog, blizzards, and high elevation.

After passing the farthest point south—where Shackleton had been forced to turn back in 1909—they halted and built their tenth and final depot at 88°25′ S. They packed a month's food supply and headed out on December 10. Because of this limited food supply, any lengthy delays due to getting lost or being trapped by a storm would be fatal.

For the next historic five days, the explorers enjoyed fine weather and an ideal surface for skiing. The summer temperatures ranged from 0° F to −18° F, and the sun radiated off a deep, loose snow cover on the quiet plateau. Anxiously, they scanned the horizon for evidence of the British—any sign of victory or defeat. When they were about six miles from the pole on December 15, Hanssen called out to the Chief to ski on ahead.

"Why should I?" Amundsen asked.

"I cannot make the dogs run without someone running ahead," his companion from the *Gjøa* days lied. He wanted to make sure Amundsen reached the pole first.

At 3:00 P.M. the drivers, who had been watching their sledgemeters, called out, "Halt!" The flag was unfurled with a

74

sharp crack in the steady breeze, and five weather-beaten fists grasped the bamboo pole as it was thrust into the snow.

Despite these gallant gestures, the victors knew they hadn't reached the exact location of the South Pole. Readings from their instruments were likely to be a mile or more off. To avoid any controversy, they planted flags every six miles to the east, west, and south. Amundsen then decided to continue on for six miles and take a second set of observations. He gave the honor of leading to Bjaaland, out of respect for the great skier, and put himself at the end to check their course.

Bjaaland consequently became the first man at the South Pole when the procession reached there on the morning of December 17. To confirm beyond any doubt that this was 90° S, they took readings using the sun every hour for twenty-four hours. There would be no question about the discovery of this pole.

Oscar Wisting poses with his dog team at the South Pole.

Taking position readings at the South Pole

That night they pitched a small tent and to the top lashed a little Norwegian flag and a pennant bearing the name *Fram*. Inside, they left some clothing, a sextant, and letters to the King of Norway and to Scott, whom Amundsen expected to arrive there soon.

After three days in the vicinity of the pole, the Norwegians set out, traveling at "night" so that the sun in its low sky position would be at their backs and not in their eyes. Struck by sunlight, the snow beacons they had built radiated like lighthouses. Everyone was in good spirits and well rested. Their only complaint was that they were too warm; the sweat poured off them. The dogs were getting fat.

As the Norwegians approached the summit of the Axel Heiberg Glacier, the British were emerging from the Beardmore Glacier on their way to the pole. This was the closest the rivals came to one another—about one hundred miles apart.

But the victors now became lost. Landmarks that Amundsen had only glimpsed through breaks in the fog during the outward journey took on a different perspective when seen clearly and viewed from the opposite direction. The difference was amazing . . . and dangerous. Luckily they were traveling to the right of their outward route and missed Devil's Ballroom altogether. They crossed Devil's Glacier in only a few hours. In addition to being first at the pole, Amundsen would never be forgiven for having such a soft time of it. He did enjoy good fortune, but his victory appeared easy because he understated it and because of the difference in professionalism between the two expeditions.

After picking up their line of cairns, the Norwegians found Butcher's Shop Depot on January 5, thanks to the sharp eye of Hanssen. This spot was completely unrecognizable from the south, as though they had never seen it before. At the depot the dogs enjoyed an extra large feed of meat. The men, however, were edgy; the place seemed haunted. As soon as the dogs finished, they loaded the sledges and were off.

The Norsemen followed the snow beacons onto the Axel Heiberg Glacier and, using ropes wound around the runners to brake the sledges, quickly made their way down as if on a long, difficult ski run. Shortly before midnight, January 7, they reached their main depot on the ice shelf at 85°5′ S. One ailing dog had to be destroyed, leaving twenty-four, exactly the number Amundsen had calculated would be left at this point.

A blizzard struck the next morning, hurrying them on their way across the Barrier. Despite frequent snowstorms, the party zipped along. Amundsen, still fearful of being beaten back with the news, decided to race. Conditions were perfect. The party also had plenty of food, so much in fact that the dogs were given chocolate as well as extra biscuits. Nearly a half-ton of food was left strewn across the ice shelf.

Amundsen, of course, had no way of knowing that Scott's group were starving and exhausted as they battled across the plateau toward the pole. It wasn't till January 16 that the British spotted a distant black speck and rushed to it. To their terrible disappointment, they found the Norwegian tent.

Amundsen's party arrived back at Framheim in the early morning hours of January 26. They quietly unharnessed the dogs and crept into the hut where the cook and the men who had been sent to King Edward VII Land were asleep.

"Good morning," Amundsen greeted Lindstrøm and asked for a cup of coffee, which he hadn't tasted in ninety-nine days.

Norwegian victory greets the British rivals at the South Pole.

Adolf Lindstrøm, cook on both Gjøa *and* Fram *expeditions, uncovered bottles of champagne to celebrate Amundsen's victory at the pole.*

Lindstrøm was stunned. "Good God, is it you?"

After the two groups had greeted one another, someone ventured the vital question: "Have you been there?"

"Yes, we've been there," Amundsen replied and there was a great hullabaloo.

Four days later, they celebrated with a farewell dinner. Lindstrøm produced bottles of champagne that he had slept with all winter to keep them from freezing.

The *Fram* had returned to the Bay of Whales on January 9, after making an important oceanographic survey of the South Atlantic. The ship brought the first news of how the world had received Amundsen's decision to challenge Scott. To his chagrin, Amundsen learned that the majority of his countrymen wanted the *Fram* ordered home. They hadn't rallied to his side, as he had expected.

Although Amundsen was showered with honors, his victory quickly soured. Johansen, who had relapsed into heavy drink-

Amundsen in his South Pole furs

ing, shot himself in an Oslo hotel room. His friends blamed Amundsen for the depression that led to the suicide. Then, less than a month later, the *Terra Nova* returned to New Zealand with the shattering news of the British polar team.

Scott and his surviving three companions had been trapped on the Barrier by one of many early winter blizzards. They were late in getting back, primarily due to the use of the ponies, and their caches of provisions were too few, too small, and too far apart to allow for any delay. On March 29, their rations depleted, the four had frozen to death in their tent, only eleven miles short of their major supply depot.

When he learned of Scott's fate, Amundsen told reporters, "I would gladly forego any honor or money if thereby I could have saved Scott his terrible death." But there was little he could do against the ghost of Scott. The old recriminations returned with renewed bitterness. The British took the romantic view, shared by others, that Scott had died of a broken heart at his defeat, which made Amundsen responsible. Scott became a hero, despite his mistakes. School children in England and other countries were taught that Scott had discovered the South Pole.

Although the accusations against him were unreasonable, they were enough to create doubt in Amundsen's own mind. What should have been a resounding victory became the source of life-long torment.

An elaborate memorial service was given Scott at St. Paul's Cathedral in London. Lincoln Ellsworth, who at the time was taking a short course given by the Royal Geographical Society, attended the service. As would be expected, he was impressed by the homage to a national hero, who had attempted what he longed to do.

During the previous year, a meeting with George Borup had crystalized Ellsworth's ambition to become a polar explorer. Borup was organizing an expedition to Crocker Land, which Peary imagined he had sighted off the coast of Greenland. Ellsworth was chosen to be civil engineer and map maker. But the day after his selection, Borup drowned trying to save the life of a friend.

The questionable qualifications of the new leader of the expedition and pressure from his father forced Ellsworth to withdraw. What Ellsworth really wanted was his own Arctic expedition, but he couldn't get the financial backing. He had to settle for a three-year assignment as a field assistant for the United States Biological Survey, reporting the distribution of animal life in the Rocky Mountain States. It was the next best thing to exploring and he enjoyed the job, particularly because of the scenic views.

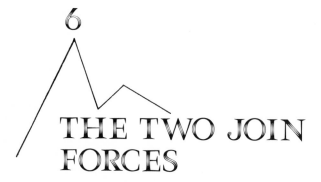

6

THE TWO JOIN FORCES

During World War I, Amundsen was invited by the French Government to visit the war front while the construction of his new ship, the *Maud,* was being completed. One evening at his Paris hotel he received a request for an interview from an American who had enlisted as a French aviation cadet to fight in the war. Being accommodating, Amundsen came down from his room to meet the caller. It was Lincoln Ellsworth.

The striking figure of the tall Viking nearly destroyed the

The Maud *navigates the Northeast Passage to reach the Arctic ice pack off Alaska.*

courage that Ellsworth had mustered to introduce himself. Amundsen's skin was weather-beaten; his gray hair had receded, leaving a bald forehead. But with a very patient attitude he sat down to listen as the American listed the training and experiences he considered to be qualifications for polar exploration. Ellsworth, who had been saddled with a desk job, begged to go with Amundsen on the *Maud*. He said he had influential friends in the States who could arrange his discharge. Wasn't there any chance Amundsen could take him?

Amundsen didn't reply immediately. He seemed to be thinking. When he spoke, his voice was edged with a tone of gentle reproof. "Isn't it a little bit late?"

Perhaps it was fortunate that Ellsworth didn't go on the *Maud* Expedition. That summer of 1918 he was knocked down by pneumonia—the illness that had killed his mother—and was incapable of doing anything arduous for five years. He might not have survived the *Maud* saga. Amundsen himself nearly didn't.

Departing Norway on July 15, 1918, the *Maud* sailed the Northeast Passage eastward along the Arctic coast of Russia to reach Alaska. Only once before had the passage been navigated. But Amundsen believed his experienced crew wouldn't have any problems. His favorite maxim was: "When it is darkest there is always light ahead." The light flickered on this expedition.

During what became a five-year ordeal, Amundsen escaped from a mauling by a polar bear and from carbon monoxide poisoning that left him with heart palpitations. He also fractured his shoulder. Because he hadn't taken a doctor along, as usual, his shoulder was improperly set by Oscar Wisting, who had studied first aid. (Wisting, one of those who had accompanied Amundsen to the South Pole, was skipper of the *Maud*.)

Dotted line approximates the route of the Maud *from Norway to Alaska via the Northeast Passage.*

Three of the Maud *Expedition members start to leave the ship on October 20, 1919, while it is icebound in the Arctic ice off the Siberian coast.*

Amundsen spent a feverish week in bed, emerging to find that he couldn't lift his right hand enough to use a pencil. But he was determined to cure himself. Several times a day he braced himself in a chair and, using his left hand, lifted his right arm as far as he could. He eventually regained the use of his right arm, although x-rays of his shoulder later revealed it shouldn't have been possible.

Once the expedition reached Alaska, the *Maud* made several attempts to enter the ice pack but failed. Amundsen and Lieutenant Oskar Omdal left the ship while it continued to probe the ice. Amundsen picked up a Junkers monoplane and, with Omdal as pilot, tried to fly across the Arctic. But the plane's skis collapsed during takeoff from Wainwright, Alaska, during 1923.

When Amundsen went to Seattle for new landing gear, an unscrupulous shipping broker convinced him that enough money could be raised to buy a seaplane for the flight. Amundsen let him take over as business manager and returned to Norway to help acquire the needed funds.

Amundsen soon discovered his new business manager was a crook and fired him. But it was too late. The explorer was left penniless. His countrymen accused him of perpetrating a hoax to get publicity and trying to make the flight without paying his creditors. His strict moral character was questioned. It was his brother Leon, however, who dealt him the greatest humiliation. Fearing what seemed to be catastrophic indebtedness, Leon sued Roald for money owed from previous expeditions. Roald declared bankruptcy, which prompted criticism that he was conspiring with his brother to defraud the creditors. Others thought that Amundsen, who had spent so much of his life seeking beyond horizons, had lost touch with reality. If this wasn't enough, doctors insisted he quit exploring because of his health.

At this crucial point—the fall of 1924—Amundsen turned to America for help and found it in the person he had rejected as a companion six years earlier—Lincoln Ellsworth. Ellsworth's father, it will be recalled, reluctantly agreed to provide $85,000 to buy two seaplanes for a transarctic flight, with Amundsen and his son as co-commanders. Although nearly everyone considered them a couple of lunatics, the two planned to fly the planes from Spitsbergen to the North Pole, where they would land and refuel one plane with the gas from the other. Abandoning the fuel-empty plane, they would fly on to Alaska. Their objective was the unexplored area between the North Pole and Point Barrow where it was believed land existed.

The expedition costs became so great, however, that they had to accept aid from the Aero Club of Norway. Because of the danger involved, the club insisted that the enterprise be limited to a reconnaissance mission to the pole and back as a preliminary to a transarctic flight. Aviation equipment at that time, it should be remembered, was as primitive as the first automobile.

Charles Lindbergh had not yet flown the Atlantic. The strength, power, range, and dependability of airplanes were still very much in question.

Amundsen and Ellsworth signed the agreement with the Aero Club, but they secretly intended to fly on to Alaska once they reached the pole. To them, the business of exploring sometimes required a "white fib now and then."

They purchased two Dornier-Wal all-metal seaplanes, which were to be flown by two outstanding Norwegian Naval lieutenants—Hjalmar Riiser-Larsen and Lief Dietrichson. The remaining crew members were two mechanics: Oskar Omdal, pilot-mechanic on the aborted flight from Wainwright, and a German mechanic working at the airplane factory, Ludwig Feucht.

Amundsen told Omdal that he was courageous to show interest in another attempt to fly the Arctic.

"So long as you don't give in," Omdal told him, "you shall always find me ready."

To Amundsen, the naval lieutenant was a "marvelous being." He seemed to have several limbs more than a normal person. He moved more slickly and thought more quickly. It was impossible to depress him.

The planes were carried in sections aboard two ships that battled 580 miles of storms and rough seas from Tromsø, Norway, to Kings Bay, Spitsbergen. Despite its isolated position, the Norwegian mining community had an ideally protected inlet. From this jumping-off point, it was only 750 miles to the North Pole.

Both Amundsen and Ellsworth were seasick during the trip to Kings Bay. The seas were so rough that hanging items, such as coats and towels, stood out from the wall. On one occasion, after a series of dizzying pitches, Ellsworth saw the veteran explorer turn pale, his forehead beaded with sweat. "You know, Captain, I don't like the sea," Ellsworth confessed.

"I don't either," replied the man who had spent thirty-two

Amundsen (right) and Oskar Omdal in flight gear at Wain-
wright, Alaska

years on the water. "It is something we have to put up with."

At Kings Bay the harbor was covered with ice, but with the aid of a local ship they managed to break open a channel to the dock. The bay ice proved to be a boon to the expedition, once the planes were reassembled. Since it offered less drag than water, the ice provided a slick runway. This enabled the flying boats to carry an additional ton of fuel. Little did the pole-seekers realize that this extra gasoline was to determine whether they lived or died.

The planes were taxied on the bay ice but never test-flown. Pilot Riiser-Larsen was confident they could take off safely. His decision may have been influenced by the knowledge that any accident would have delayed the expedition, forcing them to abandon the venture for another year. There was only a brief period during the short Arctic summer when weather conditions would make the flight possible. It was a calculated risk, as was flying *N-24* (the planes were named after their registry numbers) without a radio. Because the apparatus hadn't arrived in time, they decided to go ahead without it, even though this meant there would be no communication between the aircraft.

After waiting weeks for good weather, they finally got a break on May 21. A pale, fleckless sky with a mild breeze blowing down the fjord greeted them in the morning. The coal miners of Spitsbergen were given time off to see the departure of the six men in their clumsy polar gear and parachutes.

Because the open cockpits were exposed to the freezing air, the explorers had to be heavily clothed. In addition to woolen underwear, they each had donned a sweater, jacket, sealskin parka, two pairs of trousers, flying helmet, scarf, and gloves. They also wore oversized canvas shoes filled with senna grass, a fine hay. These boots Amundsen had innovated to keep the feet warm.

It was afternoon before the adventurers were ready and waddled to their planes. *N-25* with Amundsen, Riiser-Larsen, and

Prior to their expedition, Ellsworth (left) holds his snowshoes while Amundsen demonstrates his skis.

Feucht roared away first in a flurry of snow. The seaplane shot across the fjord ice, heading straight for a mountain glacier. Could the machine bear the tremendous excess weight? Amundsen glanced at Riiser-Larsen at the controls.

"Had he been seated at the breakfast table he could scarcely have looked less concerned," Amundsen wrote. As they neared the glacier, only the pilot's mouth betrayed any indication of his resolution and determination. Suddenly, with a mighty pull, the plane lifted into the air. A light *"Ah"* grew into a ringing shout of joy.

Not seeing their companions, they turned around and headed back. Then something blazed in the sun, glittering like gold. It was sunlight playing on *N-24*'s wings.

Seeming to be borne on mighty pinions, Ellsworth felt like a god as the aircraft banked and lifted away over a sea blanketed by fleecy fog. But unknown to anyone, rivets had been sheared off and plates loosened on the bottom of *N-24* during the take-off. The plane began leaking fuel.

For two hours they flew over an unexpectedly long stretch of fog. Only through rifts could they spot white patches of ice on the water below. Then, as if charmed, the fog slipped away under the planes, and the great white North burst forth before the awestruck visitors. The frozen ice sheet, resplendent in the strong sun, stretched three thousand feet as far as they could see, treating them to a perspective of the Arctic no one had witnessed before.

Cruising at seventy-five miles per hour, they covered a distance that would have taken a dog sledge a week to accomplish. With the aid of binoculars, they could see sixty miles in every direction, adding more than nine thousand square miles to the earth's known geography every hour. They were also proving the airplane's worth in polar work. A new era was being born, ushering out the old—the heroic age of rugged men and dogs battling the elements that had reached its culmination with Amundsen's dash to the South Pole.

Amundsen was fascinated by the ice pack. How many ships and men had been lost trying to discover its secrets? "What have you done with them?" he wondered aloud.

Except for Antarctica, the veteran explorer had never seen anything more deserted and forlorn than the top of the world. "At least I thought we might see a bear," he said.

At times, the sky and ice blended into one. Riiser-Larsen later admitted that he took a little snooze while at the controls.

A large crack in the Arctic ice sheet as seen from the air

After eight hours in the air, the planes had consumed half of their fuel. The explorers, believing they were over the North Pole, looked for openings in the ice where the seaplanes could set down. Spotting a lead, Amundsen in *N-25* waved to Ellsworth to follow and descended in a spiral.

They quickly discovered that the ice sheet had been deceptive from their flying altitude. Instead of being level, great blocks of ice were upended or piled upon each other. Pressure

93

ridges rose like fortress walls. The innocent-looking leads turned out to be gulches filled with ice floes and icebergs. Any plane would almost certainly be destroyed while attempting to land in such terrain.

Despite this terrifying sight, N-25 continued to descend. Unknown to those watching from N-24, the flying boat suddenly developed engine trouble as it disappeared into a narrow lead with surrounding hummocks and pressure ridges.

The lead N-25 dropped into was barely wide enough for the plane. Icebergs lined both sides. The slightest wobbling and it would have been all over. Any clumps would have torn the plane apart. As Riiser-Larsen zigzagged through, the wings brushed the top of an iceberg, whirling loose snow into the air. Luckily the channel was filled with slush that slowed the plane. It stopped with its nose against an iceberg. A little more speed and the nose would have been pushed in.

Thinking Riiser-Larsen had gone mad, Dietrichson flew on to search for a wider channel. He located an ice-free lagoon about ten minutes later and made a skillful landing, but the momentum of the flying boat carried it across the pool. It stopped with a thud against an ice floe six hundred feet in diameter. Water gushed into N-24's cabin.

Yanking the bell cord, the navy pilot shouted, "Omdal, Omdal, the plane is leaking like hell!"

The men jumped out, expecting a hard surface, and landed in three feet of snow.

In the strange stillness, the aliens picked themselves up in time to see a curious seal poke its head out of the water and swim within reach. Although Ellsworth had his rifle, he saw no need at the time to kill the animal. He would later regret that decision.

He and Dietrichson retrieved the sextant and artificial hori-

Route of Amundsen and Ellsworth's flight to the North Pole and return to Spitsbergen (now Svalbard)

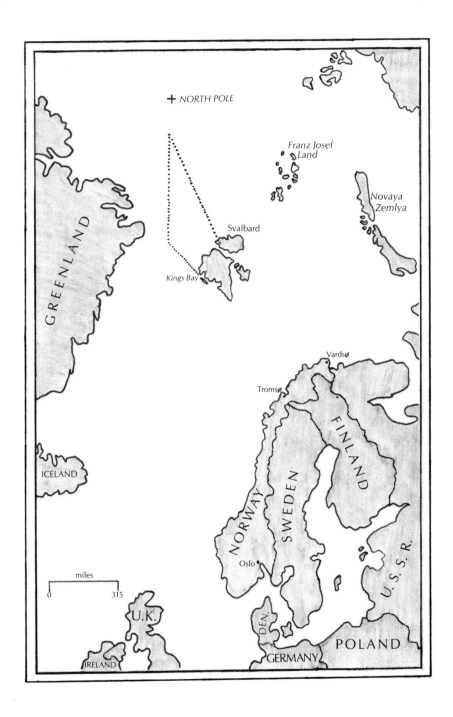

+ NORTH POLE

Franz Josef
Land

Novaya
Zemlya

GREENLAND

Svalbard

Kings Bay

Vardsø

Tromsø

ICELAND

FINLAND

NORWAY

SWEDEN

U.S.S.R.

Oslo

miles

0   315

U.K.

DEN.

IRELAND

POLAND

GERMANY

zon and took readings of their position. To their dismay, they found the planes had drifted westwardly during the flight. The men had been unaware of the subtle change in course because there were no landmarks to sight. They were 156 miles short of the pole! Compounding their predicament, they didn't know where *N-25* was.

While the mechanic pumped water from the leaking hull, Dietrichson and Ellsworth climbed the hummocks nearby and searched with binoculars for their partners. But they could see nothing in the jumbled chunks of ice. Dietrichson wondered if Amundsen had taken off again and gone to the pole without them.

"It would be just like him," muttered the pilot. But then he agreed with Ellsworth that this was unlikely. They would have heard the engines.

The two were greeted with more bad news when they returned to the plane. Omdal had found one of the engines jarred out of commission. They were nearly six hundred miles from civilization with adequate provisions for only three weeks.

After emptying most of the water from the hull, the *N-24* trio used the ice anchors to secure the seaplane to the ice floe, then moved all their supplies to a camp on the snow nearby. It was midmorning before they finished, which they could tell only by reading their watches since this was the season of the "midnight sun."

To warm themselves, the exhausted aviators melted snow to make coffee and a hot soup of pemmican. They used a little of the alcohol from the stove to fix a drink. "We owed ourselves that drink," Ellsworth wrote. But before long Dietrichson, clamping his hand to his face, shouted, "Good God! Something is wrong with my eyes!"

Ellsworth jumped to the conclusion that the alcohol had caused the problem. This was the period of Prohibition in the United States when people sometimes went blind as a result of drinking various forms of alcoholic products not intended for consumption. Ellsworth and Omdal helped Dietrichson to his sleeping bag and bandaged his eyes. The pilot's affliction fortunately proved to be snow blindness, painful but temporary.

Although they hadn't slept for more than twenty-four hours, the N-24 crew couldn't sleep. They lay in their sleeping bags, agonizing over their fate. After a brief rest, Dietrichson had enough vision to get around. He and Ellsworth climbed a nearby hill of ice and spotted N-25. Tiny black figures were working around it. Gone was the hope that Riiser-Larsen had landed safely. They tried frantically to signal their teammates by waving their semaphore flag and releasing hydrogen sounding-balloons, but the others were too preoccupied to notice. After planting a marker flag, the two returned to N-24 to help pump water while Omdal struggled with the disabled engine.

About three miles away, N-25 was upended at a 45° angle. After failing to sight their companions in N-24, Amundsen and his party had busied themselves setting up camp. They unloaded their supplies on the snow-covered ice nearby and divided the interior of the plane into living spaces.

In the afternoon of their second day on the ice, Amundsen climbed the wing of N-25 and with his binoculars sighted the sister ship. He then saw the flag atop the hill of ice. He called to one of his men to bring the similar flag carried on N-25. Ellsworth eventually spotted this signal, and the two groups began sending messages with the flags. First they tried Morse code, then semaphore. Because none of them were trained in this type of communication, it was tedious work. On each side, one man read instructions from a book while another moved the flag to the directed positions. Exchanging a simple message took them several hours.

Amundsen signaled the N-24 crew to try to save their plane as he and his men were doing. Although the job would have been accomplished more quickly if the two groups could have joined up, the three-mile journey across the ice appeared too dangerous. So Dietrichson and Ellsworth set to work digging a ramp up the ice floe in front of their plane. By dragging the aircraft up this ramp they hoped to keep it from sinking, or being crushed if the lead in the ice closed.

The job proved to be too much for three men, however. All they could manage was to pull the nose of *N-24* up the ramp, which made the aircraft safe from sinking. But the danger of the plane's being crushed in the jaws of the ice continued to mount. It was becoming colder and the wind, having changed direction, was pushing the ice together. Although this threatened *N-24,* it also moved the seaplane within two miles of *N-25.*

Since nothing more could be done, Ellsworth signaled Amundsen that his group was coming to join them. They set off on skis, dragging a sledge packed with their supplies. But after a few hundred yards, the weakened trio was forced by the deep snow and towering hummocks to abandon the sledge. They made up backpacks of fifty pounds each and pushed on.

Two hours later, although they had traveled two miles, they were only halfway to *N-25* because crevices and ridges had compelled them to take a circuitous route. A wide lead of open water confronted them at this point, and Amundsen signaled for them to return to their camp.

The ice, meanwhile, kept moving. When the *N-24* crew woke on the morning of May 26, they found themselves within half a mile of the others. The lead that had stymied them was now frozen over. Fortunately the ice hadn't shifted in the opposite direction, which it easily could have done.

Amundsen indicated he wanted them to try the crossing again. After making up backpacks that weighed eighty pounds each, the three men started out, well aware that crossing the newly formed ice would be dangerous. They wore their skis loosely fitted so they could shake them off quickly.

Reaching the lead, the men gingerly tested the precarious ice. They had to take the chance, whether the ice seemed solid enough or not. Their only hope of escape was to reach the *N-25* group and combine their resources.

Ellsworth rescues Dietrichson and Omdal.

Omdal went first. Feeling his way, he carefully pushed out one ski, then brought up the other. Ellsworth came next, using the same tactic, followed by Dietrichson. Suddenly Omdal and Dietrichson called out for help and disappeared. At the same time, the ice under Ellsworth sagged and gave way. A block of ice luckily was frozen in the lead within the American's reach. Hanging onto this, he stretched out his skis to Dietrichson and dragged the pilot through the thin ice to safety.

Turning to help Omdal, Ellsworth spotted the mechanic's head above the water. "I'm gone! I'm gone!" Omdal called out hoarsely in English as the strong current swept his legs underneath the ice. Pushing the skis ahead of him, Ellsworth wriggled toward the drowning man. After a struggle, Ellsworth, with Dietrichson's help, managed to cut off the mechanic's heavy pack and drag him onto the ice floe. Omdal was nearly unconscious, and blood trickled from his mouth where he had broken off five front teeth on the hard ice edges and ski points. His hands were cut and swollen.

Fighting for his life, Omdal followed Ellsworth and Dietrichson as they crawled from one ice block to another across the rest of the lead. Among some hummocks they were met by Amundsen and his crew, who were rushing to help them. The reunited expedition returned to Amundsen's camp, where Dietrichson and Omdal quickly changed into dry clothes and were given a shot of alcohol while cups of chocolate were being heated. Ellsworth had kept alive the hopes of the expedition by rescuing Dietrichson and Omdal from drowning. With two men gone, there wouldn't have been sufficient manpower to do the work necessary to escape.

While Omdal's hands were being bandaged, the *N-24* crew listened to what had happened to the others. Despite his condition, Omdal maintained his spirited attitude, which won Amundsen's respect.

To keep everyone from breaking down under the strain, Amundsen had set up a daily routine. Hours were fixed for eating, working, sleeping, smoking, and talking. It was a battle strategy, for they were engaged in a struggle against death by starvation. Amundsen had changed dramatically during the five days on the ice. With deep lines etched in his face from anxiety, hard work, and lack of sleep, he appeared ten years older than his fifty-two years. But his manner appeared to Ellsworth to be as cool and resourceful as ever.

After helping the *N-24* team into *N-25* to rest for the day, Amundsen's group continued working to move *N-25* out of harm's way. First, they had to chop the plane free of the sea ice that had formed around it. Then they needed to cut a ramp to haul the plane up the face of the ice block in front of the plane. Next, a level runway had to be chiseled along the top. The only equipment they had to accomplish this feat was a small ax and three wooden shovels. So they improvised. They used the plane's ice anchor as a pick and lashed their sheath knives to the ends of ski poles.

Laughing and singing during the backbreaking work, they finished the job in a day. As Feucht gunned both engines, the others pulled and pushed until they maneuvered the plane to safety on top of the ice floe. Six men had been able to accomplish what three could not.

Two days later, Ellsworth and his crew returned to their disabled aircraft. They salvaged the remaining gas and provisions and stripped usable items from the boatlike fuselage. Despite

The two downed seaplanes, the N-24 *and* N-25, *separated by half a mile of shifting ice pack*

the combination of resources, however, launching Amundsen's seaplane remained a problem. *N-25* now had twice the number of passengers it was designed to carry, and it was stranded out of the water. To escape, the explorers could chop a runway across an ice floe as rough as hummocks could make it. Or they could hope for a long lead to open up so they could get the flying boat into the water. Both options seemed impossible.

On that day, their tenth on the ice pack, Amundsen assembled everyone and defined the situation. By cutting back, they could stretch their food for two weeks—until June 15. At that time each man could either make for Greenland or stay with the plane and pray. Those who chose Greenland would have to foot it across the floating fragments of ice and use portable canoes in the water between the treacherous floes.

Day number eleven of their icy incarceration began clear and cold. Riiser-Larsen, who was always out investigating, made a joyous discovery. A long lead on the other side of their ice floe had frozen over with eight inches of ice, enough to bear the weight of *N-25*. With as much enthusiasm as his restrained Norwegian nature could allow, he informed the others.

Immediately they began the task of building a ramp down the six-foot drop to the new ice. They first made a foundation with heavy blocks of ice, which they filled in with smaller lumps and then leveled with fine ice. On top they shoveled snow and packed it down to allow it to freeze.

They finished the ramp and smoothed out fifteen hundred feet of the frozen lead in two days. On June 2, they eagerly climbed aboard the four-ton seaplane. Riiser-Larsen hit the engines. They zoomed down the ramp. *Thud!* The narrow nose of the plane was embedded in the ice. Riiser-Larsen threw the throttle wide open in hopes of lifting the plane out. But he succeeded only in breaking a channel three thousand feet long in the lead. He turned the plane around for another attempt but a thick fog suddenly set in. All they could do was wait.

Feucht was left on watch while the others retired to their cramped quarters in the plane. To keep *N-25* from freezing into the mushy water, Feucht rocked it back and forth. Inside the exhausted explorers tried to sleep to this ice-breaker lullaby.

After an hour, they heard Riiser-Larsen shouting. "Come out, everyone! The ice is closing in!" As fast as they could, the men put on their shoes and squeezed out of the plane's manhole.

They found the plane stuck in ice. Crackling and smashing sounds could be heard all around. "I expected every moment to see the side stove in like a concertina," Amundsen wrote later. A catastrophe seemed unavoidable.

Jumping up and down, Riiser-Larsen attacked the ice like a tiger. Omdal grabbed one of the tools. Amundsen and Ellsworth worked quickly to move equipment from the plane to safe ice. Once they had freed the plane, they rocked it until the ice formed underneath it.

A tall, quiet man, Riiser-Larsen seldom expressed a word of fear or hope during the ordeal. At the end of this flurry of activity, he quipped, "Another chapter for our book."

Similar chapters followed monotonously as the explorers

hacked out numerous runways, tried to take off, and felt the nose of the seaplane break through the ice. These attempts were followed by frantic periods when the ice moved in and they had to work madly to rock the aircraft free of an icy grip. Amundsen estimated that altogether they moved five hundred tons of ice during their enforced stay.

Due to the killing work and the half-rations, the men developed the haggard and drawn appearance of derelicts. They lived in their clothes and seldom washed because there was no time or fuel to waste. The sun's glare through the unremitting thin fog burned their skins black. Their confined quarters on the plane resulted in an annoying problem that was funny to all but the victim of the moment. Forced to move about bent over and drawn up as much as possible, the men often developed cramps unexpectedly. Amundsen, for instance, was working on the ice when he made a hasty jerk that gave him cramps in both thighs. Unable to move, he heard "titters and giggles and notwithstanding the infernal pain I could not do otherwise than join the general amusement." He had a robust sense of humor, although usually not when he was the butt of the joke.

The stranded aviators also began to develop what Ellsworth called polar nerves. Little things became irritating, such as Amundsen's "heroic" eating habits, which bothered everyone. Although the pemmican soup made them all thirsty, Amundsen never drank any water with it. He only chugged a mug of hot chocolate, which was served in the mornings and evenings. While the others waited for theirs to cool, he swallowed the boiling liquid as if he had a throat of asbestos. "That's good," he would say, setting down the empty mug. "There are only two times when a man is happy up here—when his belly is full of hot liquid and when he is in his sleeping bag."

Ellsworth developed an obsession over the ten malted-milk tablets each man was issued daily. Every night he planned to save one or two of the tablets for a secret feast, but he could never go to sleep without eating them all.

Feucht, who always seemed full of gloom, got on the nerves of

both Amundsen and Ellsworth. When the men ran out of tobacco, Riiser-Larsen generously shared his strong navy twist
with the others. He would judiciously whittle a few scraps of it
into each man's eager hand after the evening meal. Seemingly
unaware of what he was doing, Feucht rolled his, dropping pre-
cious flakes into the snow. This sight made Amundsen furious.

"The man does not want the tobacco at all," Amundsen told
Ellsworth. "He just takes it to bother us—so it will not last so
long."

To make the tobacco burn more slowly, the men moistened it,
which gave them all violent hiccoughs. One needed to be a hero
to smoke that tobacco, Ellsworth wrote. He didn't suggest that
it might be his father's revenge for his son's breaking his promise to quit smoking.

Poor Feucht, who had joined the expedition as a last-minute
substitute, was also careless about the crumbs from his daily
ration of three oat biscuits. Whereas the others caught the
crumbs and licked them up with their tongues, the mechanic
would let his drop unheeded. Ellsworth practiced a secret revenge by eating his last biscuit ostentatiously after Feucht had
finished. In doing so, Ellsworth convinced himself that he had
had more to eat, but he later admitted that the mechanic probably never even noticed.

To his astonishment, Ellsworth discovered that he himself ir-
ritated Amundsen, with whom he shared the pilot's cockpit.
One morning the Norwegian asked, "Ellsworth, what makes
you sigh so much in your sleep? You are always heaving those
big sighs. They keep me awake." The leader's impatience perhaps was the best indication of the severity of their predicament.

After two additional failed takeoffs, the explorers were back
in the same situation where they'd started, as June 15 loomed
closer.

The captives got a break on June 6 when the two pilots found
an ice floe suitable for a runway about a half-mile from the

plane. Building the runway would be a Herculean task; getting to it would involve a job of Arctic road building and driving the plane there. The men would have to bridge wide crevasses that separated two intervening ice floes and hack a path through a pressure ridge. But first they had to lift the seaplane out of the lead it was in and get it up on a nearby ice floe. Could they manage such a feat? "Yes!" they shouted happily at a nearby iceberg they called the Sphinx. It appeared to be bearing down on them. "Ha, ha, ha. Things are improving day by day!" But it seems they were trying to convince themselves rather than the iceberg.

The explorers swung into action and kept plugging away, even though they often regarded the situation as hopeless and impossible. Busy at work, they didn't realize the ice pack was moving. Dietrichson, who went to get something from the plane, said he thought the Sphinx was heading toward them. But the others thought he was still suffering from snow blindness.

But when the men returned to work after their skimpy meal, they realized the pilot was right. The pack was within feet of closing in. "The sight which then met us would have filled the bravest heart with despair," Amundsen wrote.

The men rushed into action. Furiously they worked to turn the plane and get it up the ramp to the top of the ice floe. They managed to do it by midnight, then fell exhausted into their sleeping bags on board.

The following morning they found the Sphinx occupying the exact spot where N-25 had been. They had escaped one more disaster. But how many more lay ahead?

They began cutting through the fifteen-foot-thick wall of the pressure ridge, which took them all day. Thankfully, the bridge-work, which involved clearing a sixty-foot path for the plane's wingspan over the crevasses, was easier. While the others held lines attached to the tail, Riiser-Larsen took the plane across the bridge. It was the crew's job to brake the plane as soon as it had cleared the chasms. Using this method, they moved *N-25* to the area where the runway was to be made.

They began the job nobody wanted to do the next morning. First, they had to shovel off two-and-one-half feet of snow, wet and heavy as lead due to the summer thaw. They then had to level a runway in the hard ice below it. By the end of the first day they had cleared only one hundred feet. At that rate the worn-out crew knew they would never finish before June 15. While struggling to turn the plane around, Omdal discovered they could move the aircraft by trampling down the snow around it. The runway could be made by simply packing down the snow rather than by trying to clear it away!

During the night it became colder and the trampled snow froze rock hard. The next day the snow became soft, then froze again at night. Omdal's idea was working. By the evening of June 14, the last of the snow had been packed down. Riiser-Larsen, after pacing off the runway, found it was 320 feet longer

Shoveling heavy wet snow, three of the explorers level a runway for N-25.

than his original estimate. They had done too much.

"If somebody offered me a million kroner for those extra hundred meters, I would not accept," Amundsen said, expressing everyone's feelings.

Ellsworth had the watch that night. As he shuffled around the plane, he saw Riiser-Larsen on several occasions pull himself up through the manhole in the plane's deck to observe the wind and temperature. While the others were "dead to the world," the pilot couldn't forget his responsibility.

In the morning, their "day of decision," Riiser-Larsen was so impatient that he woke everyone early and coerced them to gulp down their breakfast cup of chocolate and three little biscuits. Although the daily thaw was several hours away, he feared it might start earlier on that morning, the day they had to leave because of the food shortage.

The sky was full of low cloud. But as Amundsen put it: "The thickest fog would not have kept us back." They hastily un-

loaded everything not essential to their return. Clothing, half of the remaining provisions, rifles, movie cameras, canoe, and skis were dumped on the ice. It would be all over if they were forced down again.

Despite their efforts to reduce the weight of the aircraft's load, it was still questionable if they had enough gasoline to get back to Kings Bay. They had used up the safety margin of fuel in attempting to move the plane and to take off at various times.

Anxiously they took their places for the long flight. Riiser-Larsen accelerated the Rolls-Royce engines. *N-25* "trembled and shook, shivered and piped" as it bumped along the ice runway. To Amundsen, it was as though the whole of the plane's energy had been gathered for one last decisive effort. The leader, sitting beside the pilot in the cockpit, described the next few seconds as the most anxious of his life. As they gained speed, the fuselage began to career, threatening to tip them over to one side. They bounced on, reaching the last three hundred feet of the flight path that Riiser-Larsen had deemed unnecessary. It was now or never.

Abruptly the pounding and scraping stopped. As the plane lifted into the air, Omdal cheered. Amundsen felt an enormous sense of relief. Then he saw a twenty-foot-high hummock a few yards ahead. They were heading straight for it! For Amundsen the seconds seemed like "terrible hours." At the last moment the plane cleared the obstacle, missing it only by inches.

They circled above what had been their prison and waved farewell to *N-24* in its icy graveyard. From the air, they could see that their runway was on the only floe in the vicinity that could have been of any use to them.

Thick, dark fog complicated the flight south. Sometimes they flew over it, sometimes they flew under it. Riiser-Larsen occasionally skimmed the ice so Dietrichson, acting as navigator, could make drift observations. The two pilots were flying "blind." For guidance all they had was the magnetic compass, considered unreliable in the Arctic because of variations due to the influence of the North Magnetic Pole.

Hour after hour they watched the fuel gage drop lower. Would they have enough gas to get back? Were they on the right course?

With only thirty minutes of fuel left, the men began to whoop for joy. Ahead, the snowy mountain peaks of Spitsbergen pierced the horizon. The Arctic island never looked more beautiful, it seemed to the jubilant explorers. Amundsen broke open a carton of chocolate and Fuecht tossed the bars to everyone. Ellsworth wolfed down seven as fast as he could eat them.

Their celebration, however, was premature. The aileron, which Riiser-Larsen had been working with difficulty, ceased to respond. The pilot shouted the news to Amundsen. With no lateral control, they had to land immediately, despite the likelihood they would perish if forced to set down on the rough ice. They also had no survival gear, having left behind as much as possible in order to save weight. But once again fortune was on their side: a streak of black appeared below, indicating open water for landing.

They descended slowly toward the freezing water. Would they have enough fuel to keep the engines running? Lower and lower they dropped until the plane smacked safely into the water. Amundsen's estimation of Riiser-Larsen as the best pilot in Norway was justified.

The sea in Hinlopen Strait was rough. Everyone except Riiser-Larsen moved aft to lift the plane as high as possible so the pilot could maneuver it better against the high waves washing over them.

After taxiing to the shore, they moored the seaplane in a little bay. "You can call it luck if you want, but I don't believe it," Amundsen told Ellsworth. Sick from eating so many candy bars before bouncing across the water, Ellsworth wasn't in any mood to argue. He felt desperately ill.

Although they had landed safely, the explorers faced a harrowing march across the innumerable glaciers on the island to reach Kings Bay. But a few hours later, Riiser-Larsen shouted, "A sail!" They all jumped up to see a sealing vessel chasing a wounded walrus. They shouted for all they were worth, but the sealers couldn't hear them. Quickly they piled into *N-25* and, using the last of the gas, bounced across the water after the boat.

The skipper didn't recognize the six men when he took them on board. They were bearded, sunburned, and grimy. But when Amundsen pointed out his famous eagle-like profile, they were welcomed with enthusiasm. You're supposed to be dead, the astounded sealers told them.

On June 18, the six reached Kings Bay, but their triumphant return was saddened by the news that Ellsworth's father had died on June 2, the day they had made their first unsuccessful attempt to fly out of the frozen leads.

The 32-day expedition was considered successful because important scientific information had been gained about ice drift and climatic conditions near the North Pole. It also dispelled any hopes that land existed on the European side of the Arctic Ocean.

Quickly forgetting their past treatment of him, Norwegians

Safe aboard the sealer Sjøliv, *are (left to right) Hjalmar Riiser-Larsen, Oskar Omdal, Lief Dietrichson, Roald Amundsen, Lincoln Ellsworth, and Ludwig Feucht.*

Roald Amundsen's famous eagle-like profile identified him.

jubilantly welcomed their hero home, restoring Amundsen's eminence as an explorer. When the six landed in Oslo harbor, they taxied past cheering throngs, thousands of small boats, and thirteen fully manned British battleships. Guns from a nearby fort boomed a salute. Planes flew overhead. A triumphant procession through the streets of Oslo ended with a reception by the King and Queen. Their majesties conferred on Ellsworth the Norwegian gold medal for saving the lives of Dietrichson and Omdal. In his speech before the royal audience, Amundsen praised Ellsworth for saving the whole expedition.

111

Amundsen (left) and Ellsworth (far right) at their reception in Oslo

As would be expected, Ellsworth was overcome with emotion. He had made more than just a start toward fulfilling his boyhood dream of becoming a polar explorer. He was a polar hero. It was a pity his father had not lived to see it, or even to know that his son was safe.

7

ACROSS THE TOP
OF THE WORLD

Although they had barely escaped with their lives, Amundsen
and Ellsworth were determined to solve the mystery of the Far
North. They set out three weeks after their return to try again,
this time with a dirigible. Dirigible fever had struck the world
six years earlier in 1919, when a British airship, *R-34,* made the
first crossing by air of the Atlantic. Even Riiser-Larsen had become swept up by the enthusiasm and had qualified as a dirigible pilot before the flight of *N-24* and *N-25.*

Amundsen preferred the dirigible to the airplane because the airship could stay aloft longer and, despite a record of disasterous crashes, it was considered safer. A dirigible seemed just the thing in which to cross the top of the world. But Amundsen had thought a dirigible would be too expensive. To his surprise, he learned from Riiser-Larsen that an Italian model could be purchased for $100,000. Ellsworth immediately offered to put up the money, and Amundsen telegraphed the Italian dirigible designer, Colonel Umberto Nobile. Nobile traveled to Norway, and they struck a bargain. He was hired as pilot, with Riiser-Larsen as his assistant.

Everything seemed set for the new expedition. But, unwittingly, Amundsen was putting himself in a position to be exploited. The Italian dictator, Benito Mussolini, intended to use the historic flight to glorify his Fascist Italy, which he envisioned as the new Roman Empire. And the ambitious Nobile wanted to promote himself. Amundsen and Ellsworth were out of their league in dealing with such characters.

When it came time to sign the purchase contract, Nobile began making demands, including the addition of his name to the expedition title. Amundsen refused and reminded the designer that he wasn't to have any share in the command. But Nobile was set on being a star. He had no intention of playing any supporting role. Secretly he met with the president of the Norwegian Aero Club, who was overseeing the dirigible's refitting in Italy during the winter, and extracted concessions from him that the two leaders didn't know about.

On March 29, 1926, *N-1,* renamed *Norge* for Norway, started its flight from Rome across Europe and on to Kings Bay. The airship was crowded with unnecessary people, mostly guests of Nobile. The colonel also took along his fox terrier, Titina, who "wouldn't let him go alone," even though he admitted she didn't like flying at all.

The trip was particularly uncomfortable for the Norwegian members of the crew. Nobile had told them to reduce the size of

Umberto Nobile at the Norge *porthole*

their luggage and forbade them to wear their custom-made flying suits because of the excess weight. Yet the Italian crew reported aboard dressed in magnificent fur coats, carrying luggage of all shapes and sizes. Nobile had a special wardrobe that he would unveil later.

Amundsen and Ellsworth reached Kings Bay on April 12 to prepare for the *Norge*'s arrival. Instead of the ice they had encountered on their previous visit, they found open water glinting in the fjord. Snow buried the mountains and glaciers. At considerable trouble and expense, a huge, roofless hangar had been constructed to protect the *Norge* from strong winds. All of the timber had been shipped from Norway because no trees grew on the island.

During preparations for the airship's arrival and launch, the barren island was a flurry of activity and the center of world attention. Commander Richard Byrd of the United States Navy and his pilot, Floyd Bennett, with a Fokker airplane, were also on the way to Kings Bay. Would there be an aerial race to the North Pole? Many of the men involved thought so. The press certainly did, fanning the flames with sensational headlines.

Byrd arrived by ship on April 29 and announced for the first time that he was flying straight to the North Pole. Earlier, when he had asked permission to use their facilities at Kings Bay, Byrd said he intended to fly to the coast of Greenland first.

"That is all right with us," answered Amundsen, boring the American with his intense blue eyes. Although he had been deceived by Byrd, the Norwegian leader continued to advocate competition, as he always had done. "Nothing stimulates like competition, nothing encourages exploration more. It seems absurd that all should stay away from a place that someone had announced his intentions to explore," he wrote in the book about the previous flight. Undoubtedly the criticism he had received for racing Scott to the South Pole influenced Amundsen's attitude. Of equal importance was the fact that he didn't feel challenged by Byrd because Peary had already discovered

Using lifeboats, the ship's company of Richard Byrd's expedition tows the Josephine Ford *ashore through the ice floes of Kings Bay.*

the North Pole. Amundsen's interest was in flying across the Arctic.

Amundsen and Ellsworth were patient and generous explorers, both in their relationship with one another and with others. Ellsworth, however, admitted that Byrd's arrival was an annoyance, giving them "every reason to be disgruntled." Byrd's flight to the pole would divert attention away from their quest, making the public less likely to be interested in the book, lectures, and motion picture they planned to use to recoup their enormous investment. Ellsworth felt they deserved the first chance because their expedition had been planned far in advance of Byrd's, not to mention the fact that Byrd was taking advantage of their hospitality at Kings Bay.

Far more serious was the possibility that they might have to divert their expedition to hunt for Byrd if his plane should be forced down on the ice, as their seaplanes had been the previous year. Such a search would probably mean that their endeavor would have to be postponed, at a great financial loss, until the following summer.

Amundsen, however, was determined not to get embroiled in any controversy. He made sure Byrd got his flight in first. The Norwegian leader suggested a gentle slope near the dirigible's green hangar where Byrd could smooth out a runway. He instructed Bernt Balchen, a 25-year-old lieutenant from the Norwegian Air Force, to provide whatever assistance he could. After discovering Byrd wasn't carrying any survival gear in case his plane went down, Amundsen and Ellsworth provided snowshoes, and a sledge made by a carpenter taken from his *Norge* work.

You're being very generous to a rival, Byrd told Amundsen. But the Norwegian denied they were competing, a position he repeated in a pep talk to his crew. No one seemed to understand his attitude.

Byrd hurriedly made two test flights. Each time, one of the Fokker's skis broke and had to be replaced. The landing-gear

Amundsen (foreground) and Ellsworth inspect snowshoes and skis among the equipment they donated to Byrd.

strut had also been bent, and some of the Norsemen worked all night to repair it.

Three days later, May 7, the *Norge* appeared at the mouth of the fjord and floated up the bay as "sedately" as any ocean liner. Despite gusting winds, the ground crew worked the ropes and maneuvered the cigar-shaped ship safely into its canvas-covered hangar. After a very brief ceremony, the shivering Norwegian flyers, dressed in ordinary suits, rushed indoors.

Amundsen was furious at the way Nobile had treated his countrymen. But Riiser-Larsen had worse things to report. Nobile was inept as a dirigible pilot. He didn't even know how to land the airship. The worst instance had been when they arrived at Pulham, England. Nobile had refused to listen to advice about trimming and maneuvering the ship. As they approached the ground, the *Norge* shot up more than three thousand feet into the clouds before the crew could gain control. Several hours later, after many attempts, Nobile had been compelled to ask one of the special advisors on board to assist him. The landing in the presence of all the British air experts and the Crown Prince of Norway had been, in Riiser-Larsen's words, "undoubtedly the greatest manoeuvre-fiasco in air-history." As could be expected, Riiser-Larsen's friends had begun to worry about the fate of the *Norge* Expedition.

When Nobile heard of Byrd's preparations, he rushed to see Amundsen. I can have the Norge ready to go in three days! he claimed, thinking of the one engine that had been damaged during the crossing of Europe.

"Nothing doing," Amundsen told him. "We are not running a race with Byrd to the North Pole. Our job is to cross the Arctic Ocean."

Nobile was crushed. It was a lost opportunity for glory.

The following afternoon, Byrd tried again to set forth, but Bennett couldn't get the Fokker airborne. At the end of the runway the plane ran into rough ice hummocks and tipped over in a snowbank. Three hundred gallons of reserve fuel and two

The hangar, especially built for the Norge, *measured 350 feet long, 102 feet wide, and 90 feet high.*

hundred pounds of souvenirs were unloaded to lighten the air-craft, and it was taxied back to the starting point. Balchen once again had a suggestion for the Americans. If they waited until midnight, when the Arctic sun was low on the horizon, the run-way would be frozen solid, offering less resistance.

Byrd accepted the Norwegian's advice, and shortly after mid-night the *Josephine Ford* roared off into the skies over Kings Bay.

The round trip to the pole should have taken about 23½ hours, but the two flyers returned in only 15½ hours, not nearly enough time to reach their goal. Also because his sextant fell and broke, navigator Byrd had made no further observations after leaving the pole, returning to Kings Bay by dead reckon-ing. This in itself was an incredible navigational feat that should have made Amundsen and Ellsworth suspicious, particularly after their experience in flying to 88° N the previous year. But they took Byrd and Bennett at their word.

After the flight, Byrd asked Balchen, a specialist in mathe-matics, to make some computations of different positions along the route to the pole. Byrd gave him four or five problems, which Balchen worked out and returned. What Byrd did with these, Balchen couldn't say, but Byrd's charts later showed ten positions of his plane en route. When Balchen had seen these same charts in Kings Bay, however, they had contained merely a couple of scribbled notes. Had Byrd put Balchen's positions on the chart he used to prove he had flown to the pole?

Although they are remembered as being the first to fly over the North Pole, Byrd and Bennett probably got no farther than the point reached the year before by *N-24* and *N-25*. If so, the honor of first flight over the North Pole belongs to Amundsen, Ellsworth, Nobile, and crew.

While the Amundsen-Ellsworth expedition waited for a rare day of perfect weather across the entire Arctic Basin, the *Norge*'s damaged engine was repaired and glycerine added to the engine cooling system to prevent freezing. Also, extra gaso-

Amundsen (left) congratulates Byrd and his pilot, Floyd Bennett, on their return from the North Pole attempt. Ellsworth is on the right.

line tanks were installed so that the airship carried a total of seven tons of gasoline, giving it a range of 4400 miles, twice the distance to Alaska.

Weather was to be the most vital factor in determining the men's fate. Dr. Finn Malmgren, a Swedish veteran of many expeditions, had been hired to fly on the *Norge* as chief meteorologist. With two assistants working at Kings Bay to compile and relay the reports from radio stations ringing the Arctic, Malmgren was to maintain a weather map throughout the flight. His were the first intercontinental weather maps ever produced.

The weather appeared favorable, though windy, on May 11. But Nobile vacillated about making a start. Nervously clutch-

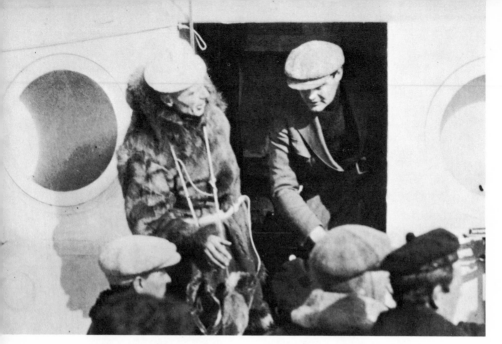

Nobile and Riiser-Larsen in the doorway of the Norge *pilothouse*

ing Titina, he announced he couldn't take the responsibility for ordering the dirigible out of the hangar.

It wasn't dangerous. The wind wasn't strong enough, Riiser-Larsen argued.

Nobile threw up his hands. "If you will take responsibility, then take her out of the hangar!"

The film of the *Norge* emerging from its enclosure consequently shows the big Norseman giving orders and Nobile standing to one side, doing nothing. He had been "supervising," the colonel later claimed.

Once the whole crew was aboard, Nobile shouted to the rope handlers on the ground, "Let go the ropes!"

"Let go the ropes!" Riiser-Larsen repeated from the starboard side, and the *Norge* slowly began to rise.

The ascent was so smooth that the snow-covered land, glinting in the sun, seemed to be drawing away from the airship. Suddenly the silence was broken by thousands of shrieking gulls and other polar birds swarming around the strange new creature in the sky. Then from below came the roar of the *Jose-*

The Norge *about to be launched at Kings Bay*

The Norge *departs Spitsbergen on its historic flight.*

phine Ford as Byrd and Bennett took off to accompany the *Norge* on the start of the journey.

More than anyone, pilot Bennett realized the danger faced by the sixteen crewmen. He had helped pick up the bodies of the twenty-four men killed in the crash of Nobile's first airship, the *Roma,* three years earlier in North America. Dipping the wings of the Fokker an hour later, Bennett turned back to Kings Bay.

Although Nobile was commander of the airship, the actual flying was done by Captain Oscar Wisting at the elevator wheel, controlling vertical direction, and by Lieutenant Emil Hörgen at the rudder wheel, determining the ship's lateral movement. The Norwegian officers were positioned in the pilothouse, the first of three compartments into which the 30′ x 6′ cabin was divided.

Nobile observed and gave instructions based on the directions of Riiser-Larsen, the navigator and second-in-command. At times, the colonel manipulated levers, releasing hydrogen to maintain the equilibrium and elevation of the dirigible. Amundsen also spent most of his time there in the pilothouse of the cabin, making his geographical observations as the *Norge* passed over virgin territory.

Riiser-Larsen had set up his navigational instruments in the center room of the cabin beside Ellsworth and Malmgren. Ellsworth, who measured atmospheric electricity with a machine installed at the request of the Curie Institute of Paris, also relieved the helmsmen and helped out in other ways. The aft compartment served as the radio room, with a corner curtained off for the toilet.

Riding in the cabin, the ten men could look up and see inside the envelope, where the rigger moved along the catwalk in rubber-soled shoes below the gas cells. The rigger periodically climbed up inside the envelope to check the girders and the gas valves. In a loft under the gas cells, most of the food—pemmican, chocolate, oat biscuits, and malted milk—was stored. There was a pound for each man for sixty days.

Nobile poses on the walkway through the rigging of the Norge.

Ellsworth takes readings aboard the Norge *next to a lineup of thermos bottles.*

Those in the cabin carried thermos bottles of coffee and tea, and cold lunches lovingly packed by Bertha, the housekeeper of the mining company's superintendent. Amundsen also had a thermos containing a concoction of grease and meatballs, which, to Ellsworth, tasted like garbage. Primus stoves were carried in the loft, in case they were forced down on the ice. But no cooking was permitted on board because of the highly flammable atmosphere of gasoline vapor and escaping hydrogen.

The other five crew members, the mechanics, rode in the gondolas with the engines or helped in the rigging.

Throughout the world, people listened eagerly to radio reports of the historic flight as the *Norge* headed north. Progress of the airship headlined across the front pages of newspapers. Would a new continent be discovered?

126

The *Norge* reached the edge of the ice pack two hours after taking off. The crew spotted a few seals, polar-bear tracks, and an occasional auk. But these signs of life quickly disappeared and there were no more in the forbidding wastes. Opening Bertha's lunches, the men found the hard-boiled eggs frozen hard as rocks and the sandwiches nearly frozen, too. After warming them in their pockets, they ate the sandwiches with the bread squeaking as they chewed. Bertha would have been crushed, had she known.

Gaining 87°44′ N, Nobile ordered the speed reduced. The *Norge* slowly descended to within a few hundred feet of the ice sheet. This was the tortured area where *N-24* and *N-25* had crashed. Omdal was called down from the rigging to join the three verterans who were marveling at the scene below. It appeared not to have changed. Even the fog was the same.

The sky began to cloud over as they continued on in periods of snow and thick fog. But the biggest danger came from ice forming on the dirigible. The aviators were forced to climb to nearly three thousand feet to escape the icing.

About one o'clock in the morning of May 12, the fog thinned, revealing the Arctic as an ice-covered sea. There was no land in sight, at least not in that area. The explorers took radio bearings, sextant observations, sun and magnetic compass readings, and made drift corrections. From all of this they knew they should reach the pole about 1:30 A.M. With his eye to the sextant, Riiser-Larsen knelt before his porthole as the time approached. The riggers and engineers were summoned to the cabin. Everyone waited breathlessly.

"Ready the flags," Riiser-Larsen said calmly. "Now we are there."

Nobile rang a bell. The engines were stopped. In the pilothouse, Wisting turned and looked at Amundsen, who was standing in the middle compartment. Amundsen said nothing to his old friend who had accompanied him to the South Pole. Wisting didn't speak either. They didn't have to. Both Norwe-

In the Norge *cabin are Nobile (top right), Wisting, Amundsen (back turned), and Riiser-Larsen (bottom right).*

gians knew they had become the first men to visit both the poles.

Begining with Amundsen, each of the three leaders dropped his national ensign. The flags, attached to steel-tipped poles, stuck upright in the ice and unfurled in the light breeze. Amundsen immediately turned and silently grasped Wisting's hand.

In keeping with a decree by Nobile, the flags Amundsen and Ellsworth had brought were not much larger than a handkerchief. But Nobile had an armful of additional banners, including pennants of the City of Rome and others, which he dumped over the side. With the colorful materials fluttering down around it, Amundsen said that the *Norge* momentarily looked like "a circus wagon of the skies." The Italian flag was so large that it got hung up on one of the engine gondolas, temporarily threatening to foul one of the propellers.

The *Norge* circled the pole at about three hundred feet. There was nothing to see but pack ice. No sign of life, not even a polar bear hurrying a cub across the floes. Had they been visitors from another planet, the explorers might have sworn life on earth was impossible and gone home.

As they pondered the floating ice, ridged at times by the pressure of shifting, Ellsworth watched Amundsen help himself to two mugs of his terrible meatball and grease "slum." Finishing, the Norwegian smacked his lips in delight.

After an hour, they set course for the other side of the world. In doing so, they changed from 2:30 A.M., May 12, Kings Bay time, to 3:30 P.M. May 11, Alaska time. The real interest of the voyage now began for Amundsen and Ellsworth as they passed over virgin vistas ranging for thousands of square miles. Maybe on this side of the pole they would find land. Peary believed he had glimpsed a continent off the coast of Greenland. Expectantly, Amundsen and Ellsworth scanned the ice floes below them. Flying at twelve hundred feet, they had an uninterrupted view of fifty miles or more in all directions during perfect visibility.

Most of the crew hadn't slept well before the flight, as would be expected. They were beginning to feel tired. They tried to sleep periodically, but it was virtually impossible due to the noise, the cold and cramped quarters, and movement around the cabin. Nobile, however, managed. According to Amundsen, the Italian slept more than anyone, although later he insisted he had slept only three hours during the entire epic. On this flight, Amundsen and Nobile were to agree on very little.

At 88° N 157′ W, the *Norge* crossed the hypothetical Ice Pole, sometimes called the Inaccessible Pole, around which all of the Arctic ice drifts. To those who were first to see it, the area ap-

Amundsen wrapped himself up to keep warm in the cabin of the Norge.

peared as a chaotic sheet of ice, full of barricades and ridges but without any leads in the ice. Surface travel of any kind would be impossible.

The expedition ran into trouble two hours later, twenty-four hours from Kings Bay and halfway to Point Barrow. Fog. It started as scattered pools below them, then thickened until it engulfed the ship. The fog lasted throughout most of the remaining flight. Only occasional breaks allowed the crew to observe the sea and ice below.

The fog brought such poor visibility that the explorers had only radio signals to guide them. Settling on the dirigible, the fog condensed and turned into ice—perilous ice. The ice broke loose in large chunks and, sounding like little explosions, was whirled by the propellers into the canvas. The delicate covering was torn in several places and couldn't be mended! The rigger shouted down to the crew in the cabin.

But the icy projectiles threatened an even greater peril. They might pierce the gas cells, causing an irreplaceable loss of hydrogen. Or they might break a propeller blade, inflicting serious damage if it struck the envelope.

After an hour in the fog, the radio reception grew increasingly fainter. Abruptly, it stopped altogether. The aerial, a wire 450 feet long trailing behind the cabin, was coated with ice. It looked like a porcelain rod. Although the aerial was wound up and cleaned several times, it froze again as soon as it was dropped back. Five spare aerials eventually broke under the weight of the ice.

Without the radio, the aviators no longer had any weather reports or bearings for navigation. Their last report had come from the United States Government station in Alaska. Now they were at the mercy of an unreliable magnetic compass and a sextant that could be read only when they were able to see the sun.

Around the globe, various governments put naval vessels in the region on alert, and an anxious world waited for word from the silent airship.

Meanwhile, the *Norge* battled on, buffeted by snow squalls, intensifying winds, and hurling chunks of ice. As if sensing the danger, Titina, who had slept most of the way, jumped to the floor. She began whimpering, which didn't help the deteriorating morale.

Nobile sought Malmgren's help. The meteorologist began making tests to determine the amount of ice forming on the dirigible at various heights. With these readings, a course could be navigated through the fog with the least danger from the accumulating ice. The *Norge* sometimes flew high as a result; at other times, it nearly grazed the ice pack. Despite this tactic, ice formed on the bow, tipping the nose of the airship downward. They were in danger of crashing. Quickly the gasoline ballast was shifted to balance the weight, and the *Norge* leveled off.

When Riiser-Larsen eventually got a shot at the sun with his sextant, he discovered the *Norge* was only twenty-one miles west of the meridian chosen for their route south from the pole.

Then the weather began to improve as they neared the Alaskan coast. If only their luck would hold . . .

About three hours later, Riiser-Larsen, who had been studying the horizon with his binoculars, called out, "Land off the port bow!"

The others hurried to the portholes. Taking out their field glasses, they scrutinized what appeared as a faint black line some thirty miles beyond a sheet of ice that was clinging to it. Land! It was barely distinguishable, but it was there. The Arctic had been crossed, and man knew, more or less, what the top of the world looked like. There was no new land, only ocean and ice. The flight also gave the first visible proof that the world was indeed round.

The *Norge* soon floated over the frozen beach. It was 8:30 P.M., May 12, nearly two days after the dirigible had left Kings Bay. Although the explorers could calculate the local time, they had difficulty determining exactly where they were. Visibility was limited. Their charts of the area didn't agree with the contours of the coast. Amundsen, who had been to northern Alaska before, said he thought the area looked like Point Barrow country. The wisest policy, it was decided, was to sail southwest down the Alaskan coast. When they found some identifiable features, they could fix their position and proceed on to Nome, their destination.

With gale-force winds beginning to push the *Norge* along faster, the expedition sped on into thickening weather. They were flying low, between 600 and 750 feet, in order to distinguish the wintry shore from the frozen sea. About an hour later, the crew spotted a few Eskimo, gaping at the strange object in the sky. What was it? their attitude seemed to say. A flying seal? The devil?

The dirigible then passed over a caribou farm, huts, and a red-roofed schoolhouse. Amundsen and Omdal immediately

Dotted line shows route of the Norge *across the Arctic.*

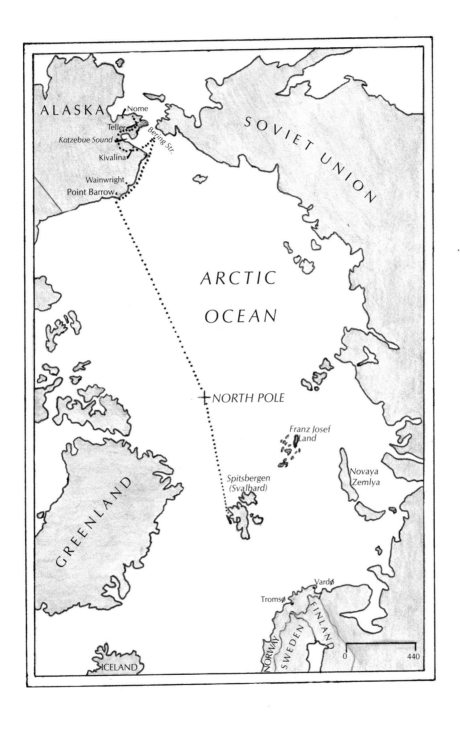

ALASKA

Nome
Teller
Kotzebue Sound
Kivalina

Wainright
Point Barrow

Bering Str.

SOVIET UNION

ARCTIC

OCEAN

+ NORTH POLE

Franz Josef
Land

Novaya
Zemlya

Spitsbergen
(Svalbard)

GREENLAND

Vardø

Tromsø

NORWAY

SWEDEN

FINLAND

ICELAND

0   440

recognized the little place. Wainwright! They knew every house, particularly Maudheim, which they had built in 1922 during their first attempt to fly across the Arctic. The current residents, gathered on the roof, cheered as the airship passed overhead. Nearby, other villagers shouted and waved their hats. Amundsen had returned . . . in triumph!

Finding Wainwright, however, didn't help the expedition much, although the news of the historic crossing could be telegraphed to the waiting world. The *Norge* was compelled to continue on, flying so low in the murky weather that capes and headlands seemed to jump up to meet the crew. During the night, the airship pitched and rolled in winds that reached hurricane force. Icing again threatened the ship.

The expedition had two choices: fly over land and lose the ice but risk crashing into a mountain, or head out to sea and take the chance of being forced down due to the accumulating ice. They faced possible disaster, whichever gamble they took. Deciding to stick to the coast, they climbed to a higher altitude and continued on blindly. At one point, while over land, their precarious situation was dramatized by the radio antenna's scraping on a mountaintop.

After the brief hours of darkness, the crew discovered that the dirigible had gathered too much ice. The men riding in the rigging had to scramble to the extreme end of the keel to trim the ship. Although they were saved once again, they had no idea where they were. They believed they had been blown off course and were south of Nome. But, as they soon discovered, they were actually over the Bering Strait, heading toward Siberia!

Turning around, they descended and flew as low as six hundred feet to keep sight of the turbulent sea as they returned to the Alaskan coast. It was a rough ride. At times, the winds tossed the airship up or down 150 feet. Low clouds periodically blocked the view. Once more sensing the danger, Titina stalked the cabin, whining, with her tail between her legs.

The storm showed signs of abating about 10:30 A.M. Through

Omdal looks out from the rigging of the Norge.

Nobile and Titina photographed in the dismantled cabin of the Norge.

a break in the white fog, a group of igloos appeared on the flat, snow-cloaked coastline. Amundsen thought the place was Kivalina. They steered over some Eskimo standing outside their hut and tried to hail them. Rather optimistically, they hoped that they might inquire directions from the awestruck natives. Of course, the Eskimo didn't understand what was being shouted and gestured from the sky. And it was too windy to try again.

Riiser-Larsen suggested that they land. Nobile, however, wanted to continue on to Nome, where their reception was waiting. It would be easy, he argued, if they kept low along the coast. Amundsen and Ellsworth didn't overrule him, and he prevailed.

First, Riiser-Larsen wanted to verify their position. He wanted to make sure they weren't flying to some other part of the world again. Nobile took over the controls, guiding the *Norge* up above the fog to an altitude of nearly four thousand feet. But the sun was high overhead at this time of day, which prevented the navigator's using his sextant from the cabin porthole. So the indomitable Norwegian slung his instruments around his neck and climbed the ladder in the bow of the balloon to make his observation on the icy flat top of the envelope! This, however, was only a single reading. They needed another, such as a radio transmission from Nome and another known location to coordinate their longitude and latitude.

Riiser-Larsen returned to their cabin none too soon. Forgetting to watch the gas pressure, Nobile had taken the dirigible too high. The hydrogen, warmed by the sun, quickly expanded, threatening to burst the envelope. They had to descend quickly, but couldn't because the airship was down by its stern, its nose pointing up. Nobile spun the elevator wheel in an effort to bring the nose down, but the control failed to respond. He panicked.

"Run fast to the bow! Run fast to the bow!" he screamed, wringing his hands.

Everyone except Nobile and the two helmsmen rushed forward into the nose of the dirigible, dragging cases of pemmican and cans of gasoline. Wisting then turned the vertical helm hard, the ship tilted, and they went down just as fast as they had risen. The men had to scramble aft to keep the cooling ship from going into a nose dive.

It had been the most dangerous hour of the voyage. The *Norge* had risen to 5400 feet in a few minutes, then plunged down. With control regained, the dirigible leveled off at 600 feet. Meanwhile, the ship had been blown inland and had to make its way back toward the sea against strong head winds. In order not to lose their direction again, the crew followed the coastline, flying low under the fog despite the dangerous, often hilly terrain. The antenna was snapped off on a hilltop and had to be replaced again. At other times, they were threatened by the rough sea ice along the shore.

Because Nobile didn't consider any of the Norwegians sufficiently expert to pilot the ship under challenging conditions, he decided to take over the elevator wheel himself. He stationed Riiser-Larsen at a porthole to shout, "Up!" whenever they approached an obstacle. But the colonel soon became distracted and forgot he had changed direction. The *Norge* plummeted toward disaster once again. Standing like a man in a trance, the skipper appeared unaware of the impending peril.

Riiser-Larsen sprang into action. Pushing the colonel roughly aside, he grabbed the wheel and spun it around. The men rushed to the cabin portholes to see if the rear engine gondola would clear the surface. It did, but only by inches.

The explorers at this point were exhausted, their nerves frazzled from the long, demanding flight. Some had begun to hallucinate. Omdal thought he saw a famous mountain landmark. The others looked, but there was no mountain there. On another occasion, one of the crew believed he saw an army of men and horses charging across the frozen surface.

About two o'clock, the ice was cleaned off the antenna. The radio operator, Captain Birger Gottwaldt, picked up a radio bearing from the station in Nome. He reported that the weather

Norge crewmen listen in hopes of picking up radio signals to help verify their position.

was calm there and a group of men were waiting to help land the dirigible. The world, too, was waiting, since nothing had been heard from the *Norge* in some time. Many still feared the expedition had been lost.

Continuing south, the *Norge* probably crossed the eastern end of Kotzebue Sound, but no one aboard could be sure. The first identifiable landmark was the sinuous Serpentine River, its frozen curves unmistakable. Believing everything was under control, Nobile collapsed in Amundsen's armchair and slipped his legs into the fur sleeping bag. Titina had been cuddled up there for most of the flight.

Nobile slept for four and one-half hours. He believed the crew could easily find the way to Nome from the river by flying along the coast. Undoubtedly, the Italian's exhaustion was compounded by his emotional nature as well as by stress and lack of rest. (He later claimed to have stayed awake most of the time due to supreme will power.) Nobile must have been worn out indeed to sleep through the stormy weather that followed. At times, the *Norge* stood still in squalls.

Following along the coast, they passed Cape Prince of Wales at about five o'clock. Whenever they veered out to sea, conditions were worse than over land. The airship was tossed up and down like a ball by strong winds that also drove the craft sideways.

A half-hour from their destination, Riiser-Larsen woke the skipper. "Getting near, sir."

The sky was black above. A persistent gale pitched the *Norge* dangerously, impeding its progress. Below, the men saw dark masses of huts and a three-masted boat lying frozen on its side. Amundsen, standing beside Wisting at the helm, acted as guide because of his familiarity with the region. Still, he couldn't recognize this village, although he knew it wasn't Nome. The place was too small, and there wasn't any tall telegraph mast.

Although they were short of their destination, Nobile decided the threatening weather and the condition of the crew made it necessary to land before it became impossible for them to control the ship. The men hurried to make ready. The riggers improvised a heavy anchor from two of the ice anchors and six hundred pounds of heavy objects, while the *Norge* hovered over the village's frozen bay.

"Prepare to drop the landing ropes!" Nobile called up to the rigger.

Worried about Nobile's judgment, Amundsen asked Riiser-Larsen his opinion about the safety of the site. Riiser-Larsen replied that it would be safe unless the wind was strong. He suggested a precautionary measure he had been taught at dirigible school in England. By knocking out the canvas sides of the

139

cabin, the men could jump clear if the landing became too violent.

They can't do that! Nobile, who had overheard the navigator's advice, shouted. He later accused Riiser-Larsen of panicking and making a wild suggestion that endangered the lives of the crew.

At five hundred feet, the anchor was lowered. As it hit the ice, a gust of wind suddenly hurled the ship toward the shore, dragging the anchor along. The men hung on for their lives. Just in time the wind let up, and the anchor took hold in the ice. If the wind hadn't slackened, the story would have been entirely different, rivaling the fiery crash of the *Hindenburg*.

Nobile ordered the engines stopped. As hydrogen was released from the gas cells, the *Norge* slowly began to sink. On the ground, the villagers ran to grab the ends of the dangling landing ropes. When Nobile pulled the rip cords, the crew leaped out and joined the rope handlers. Slowly the bag, sheathed in a ton of ice, sagged into its tubular skeleton and the dirigible came to a rest, looking like a collapsed balloon, about a hundred yards from the nearest cottage.

The time was 8:30 P.M., May 13, seventy hours and forty minutes after leaving Spitsbergen. At an average speed of 45 mph, they had covered an estimated 3390 miles, about 278 miles less than the distance between New York and Paris.

Surprisingly, the villagers were calm, greeting the explorers as if airships pulled in there every day.

"Where in the world are we?" the crew wanted to know.

"In Teller," came the reply.

Teller? That was one hundred miles from their destination!

Even Ellsworth, who had been there before, hadn't recognized the place. But after landing, he recalled standing on that beach twenty years earlier. He had looked out across the unknown, wondering what lay beyond the horizon. He now knew what was out there. Soon, the rest of the world would know, too. He and Amundsen walked ashore together.

The Norge *is deflated at Teller.*

For the two leaders, their boyhood dreams had come true. Amundsen's career as an explorer had been crowned with success in gaining what he called "practically the last of the great possible achievements." Ellsworth's career was now firmly established, catapulting him on toward those last "great possible achievements."

By the time the crew secured the airship, hot meals were prepared in the village and accommodations readied for the weary men. Riiser-Larsen was given two charming rooms. One, where he deposited his luggage, looked out to the sea; the other faced the land. When asked by his host if he would like to invite one of his companions to take the vacant room, the good-natured pilot invited Nobile. The flight was over. They had been successful, and he as well as Amundsen wanted to forget any misunderstandings or discontent.

141

That evening the Italian, pouting like a child, arrived at a dinner party for the expedition. Although he was hours late, he demanded something to eat and then ate in morose silence. He was brooding over the lack of precedence and attention paid to him. He had begun to take his pretentiousness as actuality. Not only was he a high-ranking officer but also a major explorer. When Riiser-Larsen returned to his room at midnight, he found Nobile had picked up his luggage, thrown it in the other room, and taken the room facing the sea. Nobile was lucky that the big Norwegian had a high boiling point.

Because the telegraph wasn't working at Teller, the two commanders rented a launch and proceeded to Nome, after instructing Captain Gottwaldt to repair the equipment. When Gottwaldt got the Teller apparatus working, Nobile began sending out press reports. In Nome, meanwhile, the leaders were working on the first installment of the exclusive story for American newspapers. Furious, Ellsworth wired the Norwegian Aero Club, asking them to protest the Italian's statements. But the news story had become public property by this time, nearly causing a breach of contract for Amundsen and Ellsworth with the American newspapers.

More telegrams flashed between the Aero Club and the expedition leaders. To their utter dismay, Amundsen and Ellsworth learned that the club president had made changes in the expedition contract without telling them. Nobile's name had become an official part of the title, making it the Amundsen-Ellsworth-Nobile Transpolar Flight.

But that was only the beginning. Nobile sent to Ellsworth a confidential letter in which he listed his complaints. By appealing to Ellsworth, who had a much more agreeable nature than Amundsen, Nobile hoped to split up the united front of the two leaders in such a way as to favor his efforts to claim a major share in the undertaking. However, he underestimated Ellsworth's character and dedication to Amundsen. The American resented the letter and immediately showed it to his friend.

Amundsen enjoys a relaxing smoke after the Norge flight.

Nobile's resolve, of course, was not shaken. When Amundsen arranged for a boat to bring the crew to Nome, Nobile telegraphed the United States Coast Guard and requested a cutter. On it he made a separate and ostentatious entry into Nome with his five countrymen.

The best hotel rooms available in town had been rented by the commanders for all of the men, but Nobile felt the arrangements were below his dignity as an Italian officer. He selected the largest hotel and, although it was closed for the winter, obliged the facility to be opened for him to take up residence in solitary grandeur.

Ellsworth eventually persuaded Nobile to air his grievances in a conference with Amundsen and himself. In addition to being left out of the authorship of the newspaper articles, the Italian complained that the Norwegian crewmen had insisted on having a party by themselves to celebrate a Norwegian national holiday while they were waiting in Teller. Nobile was insulted because he hadn't been invited. But he had suffered greater indignation when the crew later were sweating to pull the *Norge* ashore. An onlooker, seeing Nobile standing with his hands in his pockets, had exclaimed, "Why don't you get to work?"

Nobile was incensed that the leaders hadn't shown him the consideration to which his rank entitled him. Although Amundsen explained that he was a member of a private expedition, not a national undertaking, the colonel left the meeting dissatisfied. Amundsen was technically correct, but national honor was very much involved, even his own, as the renaming of the dirigible demonstrated.

A few days later, Nobile asked for another conference, during which he demanded to be recognized as one of the expedition leaders as well as co-author of the book and newspaper stories. When Amundsen reiterated that he was merely the airship's commander, the Italian burst into a tirade, accusing them of callously treating him like an ordinary crew member. Perhaps the colonel should have been given greater importance, but historically the masters of expedition vessels were seldom credited or remembered on a basis equal with the leader. Take Byrd, for an example. His pilots on flights to both the North Pole and the South Pole have remained virtually unknown.

Nobile claimed to have experienced a vision in which he conceived the idea of the flight. He had designed the ship for this daring exploit and then joined with Amundsen and Ellsworth. "I have given my life to this expedition—I had the whole responsibility of the flight!" he shouted.

This was too much for Amundsen. What a pitiable spectacle you would have made on the ice if the *Norge* had been forced down! he told the Italian. Amundsen concluded with the assurance that he would never recognize Nobile's claim that he was a leader of the enterprise.

Amundsen and Ellsworth on a dog sledge in Nome

Remarking that he was sick of the whole affair, Nobile shrugged hopelessly at the veteran's stinging rebuke. But he had no intention of giving up. With the help of a local priest, Nobile promoted himself so successfully that when a public banquet was given in Nome to honor the entire expedition, Amundsen and Ellsworth weren't invited!

When the waterways were passable on June 17, the expedition sailed to Seattle with the boxed-up dirigible aboard. Nobile's subordinates confided to the Norwegians during the trip that they disapproved of their leader's conduct. "We sympathize with you in this matter, but what can we do?" Amundsen said he admired the Italian crewmen and asserted there was never any ill-feeling between him and them.

A boat with a large Italian flag greeted the victors as they entered Seattle harbor ten days after leaving Nome. The harbor was jammed with launches and jubilant crowds singing *"O Sole Mio."* Stepping to the rail to acknowledge the reception,

145

*(Left to right) Riiser-Larsen, Amundsen, Ellsworth, Nobile, and
Titina after their arrival in Seattle*

Amundsen and Ellsworth were perplexed when nobody noticed
them. Perhaps the reason was that they looked like ordinary
miners. Because of Nobile's insistence that no extra clothes be
carried on the flight, they'd had to pick up wool shirts and trousers in Nome after shedding their flying gear.

Then they saw Nobile, glittering in his military uniform, on
the bridge, Titina barking excitedly at his feet. Promoted to
general by Mussolini during the voyage to Seattle, Nobile lifted
his arm in the Fascist salute. Boatloads of Italian-Americans,
sent by the local Italian consul to greet him, cheered wildly.

After a reception, the expedition disbanded. Amundsen and
Ellsworth traveled across the United States by train to New
York. They were paraded down Fifth Avenue before leaving for
similar honors in Europe. When Norway feted them, Ellsworth
was honored as a foster son. He was called a "modern viking"
and "one of ours." In addition to receiving medals, he had a
mountain in Spitsbergen named for him.

Nobile, who had planned to equip an airship in Japan after
the flight, received orders from Mussolini to embark on a lec-

146

ture tour of the "Italian colonies" in the United States. With elaborate fanfare, the general visited thirteen cities. Altogether, twenty-four cities, including New York, made Nobile an honorary citizen. Italy awarded him its highest decoration, the military Order of Savoy. France conferred the Legion of Honor.

By this time Nobile had gone so far in distorting the truth that the gentle Ellsworth felt compelled to issue a statement. In fairness to the men who did most of the flying of the *Norge,* Ellsworth said it should be known that Nobile had actually flown the airship for three short periods only and at no time had acted as navigator. "In fact, I doubt if he understands navigation."

Nobile countered with his own version, alleging he had done all the preparations for the flight and everything had depended on him during it. Ellsworth "was just a passenger whom I took on board at Spitsbergen and left at Teller." Italian newspapers, meanwhile, continued to fan the flames by announcing that the Italian crew had done all the work while the Norwegians had slept on the *Norge.*

When Amundsen returned to the United States in November of 1926, he discovered that Nobile was making a lecture tour of the country for his own profit, due to the crowning mismanagement of the Aero Club. Amundsen was faced with the task of trying to recover the outstanding debts of the expedition after Nobile had scooped the cream from the news event for himself. The Norseman and Nobile never saw one another again, although Amundsen's fate ultimately was to be determined by the general.

During one of the happier moments of Amundsen's final American visit, he was entertained by his friend Ellsworth. "Do you know I have adopted many of your ways," the Norwegian said. "I have learned to smoke my pipe in bed of evenings and have written Montreal for fifty pounds of that French-Canadian tobacco you smoke and I only eat two meals a day now. I never have the tight feeling around the belt any more."

Autographs on cloth of some Norge *crew members*

At a little private dinner in Washington, D.C., Amundsen and Ellsworth, along with Byrd, inaugurated the Polar Legion, probably the most exclusive club in the world. Members had to be leaders of expeditions that had reached either pole. Although they were dead, Peary and Scott were voted in as charter members and club pins were sent to their widows.

Byrd announced at the dinner that he intended to fly to the South Pole. Later, Amundsen said to Ellsworth, "I don't understand such a thing. I was there, Scott was there—there is nothing more to find. Why should anybody want to go to a place where somebody else had already been?"

To Ellsworth, that was Amundsen's whole attitude toward exploring.

8

EPITAPH FOR
A VIKING

Having convinced himself that he was a great explorer, Nobile began to plan an Arctic adventure of his own. He wanted to survey coastal areas of the Arctic Ocean off Siberia, Canada, and Greenland. If any land remained to be discovered, he wanted to be the one to find it. He also proposed to moor an airship at the North Pole, lower scientists to the ice, and gather scientific data.

Nobile promoted the flight as a daring exploit, but few people, including Mussolini, were interested in what appeared to be a repeat performance of the *Norge* expedition. The deluded general asked Ellsworth to join him, but the American understandably refused. However, two years later, Nobile succeeded in gaining enough financial backing to build a modified version of the *Norge* which he named the *Italia*.

The new dirigible left from Kings Bay on May 23, 1928, and flew to the North Pole via the Greenland coast. After circling the pole on May 24, the expedition headed back to Spitsbergen. Nobile was warned by one of his officers that the ship was responding suspiciously. The general ignored the advice.

About 180 miles north of Kings Bay, the next day, the ice-heavy dirigible suddenly began to fall. This time there was no Riiser-Larsen aboard to save the ship. It smashed into the rough pack ice. The wind carried off the battered dirigible and six horrified crewmen who were clinging to the wreckage. The *Italia* was last seen as a column of black smoke on the foggy horizon. Nobile and nine others were scattered on the ice, along with Titina. The little dog, happy to be on the ground, raced around barking and rolling in the snow.

Nobile, wearing a sweater and thin trousers, had broken his arm and his leg. In a weak voice he exhorted his men to accept their fate and trust in God. "Long live Italy," he concluded. Then, insisting he was about to die, he instructed the first officer, Adalberto Mariano, to take care of the others and stuck his head in a sleeping bag. But momentarily he peeked out when Malmgren, whom he had persuaded to make the trip, announced he was going to drown himself.

"No, Malmgren! You have no right to do this. We will die when God has decided. We must wait," the general argued, and the meteorologist sat down.

Taking account of their situation, the dazed men discovered that the motor mechanic foreman was dead and Natale Cecioni had a piece of bone protruding through the skin of his broken leg. The radio was recovered intact, but it didn't seem to be sending their desperate SOS signals.

The ill-fated Italia *is launched.*

Malmgren, the only one with actual Arctic experience, shot a polar bear. The carcass provided four hundred pounds of meat, enough to feed the survivors for several weeks. But the immediate problem was insurrection. Mariano and the third officer, Filippo Zappi, no longer trusted their leader's judgment and insisted on marching across the ice to reach nearby islands. Unlike Amundsen, Nobile hadn't learned any leadership techniques. He didn't know how to make his men agree among themselves as well as with him. Pressured by the two naval officers, he gave in, permitting them to take Malmgren along as guide.

When it was announced to the world that radio contact had been lost with the *Italia,* Amundsen was attending a banquet to honor George Wilkins and Carl Eielson, who had recently flown by airplane from Point Barrow to Kings Bay. A rescue operation had to be organized quickly, the dignitaries gathered at the Royal Norwegian Yacht Club agreed. The group became silent as everyone looked at Amundsen, who had published a scathing indictment of the Italian in his memoirs the previous year.

"I'll come right away," the 54-year-old veteran promised.

It was a difficult situation, he told reporters who were pressing for his comments. There was no indication of the *Italia*'s position. Because of the ice, a ship could search only a limited area. And the summer thawing made it hazardous, if not impossible, for a plane to land on the ice. But he added reassuringly, "All that can be done, will be done."

Considering his age and the number of experienced aviators on hand, Amundsen didn't have to get involved. But he didn't want to be seen as responsible for another explorer's death. He also feared he might be jeered as a coward for not making the flight. As a result, he was pried out of retirement to help rescue the man he disliked the most.

The Italian ambassador asked the Norwegian Government for help, even though the Italian Government refused to concede that the *Italia* had crashed. Amundsen was among those Arctic experts called together to plan the operation. Everyone assumed Amundsen would be placed in command of the mission, which prompted Mussolini to inform the Norwegians that their help wasn't needed. The dictator disapproved of Amundsen because he considered the explorer's accusations against Nobile as an insult to Italy. To avoid offending *Il Duce,* the Norwegian Government dropped Amundsen and went ahead with Riiser-Larsen in charge.

Amundsen felt betrayed once again by his countrymen. Having publicly announced he would go to Nobile's aid, his honor demanded that he do so. He was barely solvent, however, and had to beg for support to organize a private rescue mission.

In an interview with an Italian reporter who visited the restless explorer, Amundsen reiterated that in such a situation personal resentments must be set aside. His attention was diverted momentarily by a model of the *N-25* on his desk. With a distant look in his eyes, Amundsen added, "If you only knew how splendid it is up there! That's where I want to die; and I only hope death will come to me chivalrously, that it will overtake me in the fulfillment of a high mission, quickly, without suffering."

On June 8, the *Italia* castaways managed to get their radio working so that at least their position was known.

Meanwhile the search had become an international scramble for prestige. In addition to Norway, Sweden and Russia launched rescue efforts. France and the United States offered assistance, too. Unable to decide on a plan of action, Italy finally accepted Norwegian assistance and sent one seaplane to help out.

There were now six nations involved in what became the largest international rescue ever mounted. Altogether, fifteen hundred men, twenty-two planes, eighteen ships, and two dog teams were mobilized in the effort. Ellsworth also offered to help, but there appeared to be more than enough rescuers on the scene.

In Paris, a Norwegian businessman convinced the French Government of the prestige to be gained by aiding Amundsen. The French as a result provided a Latham seaplane, serial number 47, which its pilot, René Guilbaud, was planning to use in an attempt to cross the Atlantic. Although the long-range model was relatively untested, Amundsen, eager for action, accepted it.

Hundreds of offers to accompany Amundsen poured in, but he decided to use the four-man crew of the Latham 47, who were familiar with the plane. He also enlisted Leif Dietrichson because of his polar knowledge.

On June 16, a crowd gathered at the Oslo train station to see Amundsen off to meet the plane, which the Frenchmen were flying to the Norwegian city of Bergen.

"Come back! Norway needs you!" someone shouted.

Amundsen replied, "Our machine is speedy."

As the train pulled away, he stood at the window waving slowly until the throng disappeared from sight. On that same date, twenty-five years earlier, he had set off to conquer the Northwest Passage.

It was evident that the Latham 47 was overloaded and unsuited for the Arctic by the time Amundsen and his companions landed at Tromsø, Norway, two days later. Although he knew it was foolhardy to continue, the Norseman couldn't turn back. To do so would have made him appear unwilling or afraid to make the flight. Three other seaplanes at Tromsø—one each from Sweden, Finland, and Italy—were bound on the same mission. When the Swedish pilot suggested they wait a day and cross the dangerous Barents Sea together, Amundsen refused. Since some twenty other planes were involved in the rescue, it was now a race to reach the survivors first.

That afternoon, June 18, the Latham 47 taxied across the harbor. Spewing spray in its wake, it took off into the bright light of a clear summer day. A short while later, the plane disappeared into a fog bank to the northwest. The plane carried a fuel supply for thirty flight hours.

Two days passed. Nothing was heard from the Latham 47. On June 22, the Italian Government agreed to release to Riiser-Larsen the *Braganza,* a plane-carrying ship chartered for the rescue of Nobile. Riiser-Larsen was anxious to start searching for Amundsen since Nobile had been located. The Italians also ordered two of their pilots to begin looking for the missing Viking. But no all-out search was launched because everyone believed it was more important to pick up Nobile's inexperienced crew. If Amundsen were alive, he was capable of taking care of himself and his companions; if not, there was no need to hurry. Some people speculated that Amundsen might have by-passed Kings Bay and gone straight on to make the pickup.

The following evening, two Swedish aviators landed at the *Italia*'s crash site, which looked more like a garbage dump than a camp. Because of the size of the Fokker airplane, there was room for only one passenger. Nobile wanted the injured Natale Cecioni, who had been one of the *Norge* crew, to leave first. But the Swedish pilot insisted the general go first, arguing that Nobile would be more useful directing the relief operation from the base ship.

After his comrades agreed, Nobile, carrying Titina, was helped to the plane. His men watched as he flew off to medical attention and safety, leaving behind Cecioni with his compound fracture and Felice Trojani, laid up with a fever in the tent.

At the base ship, Nobile found himself unwanted. He had no useful information. Even his government had little faith in him, cabling that an officer of lower rank was to take command. Interviews with Nobile were prohibited. He became virtually a prisoner, although this didn't deter him from making suggestions. The news media around the world had a field day, reporting that the Fascist general had abandoned his companions but saved his dog.

As the fiasco continued, the Russians arrived on the scene. Their icebreaker, *Krassin,* entering the open sea north of Norway on its way to rescue the stranded Italians, was greeted by fishermen in small boats shouting, "Save Amundsen! Bring back Amundsen!" Although the Russians did have orders to help find the missing Norwegian, the rescue of the *Italia* survivors was their priority.

Hampered by a broken propeller and heavy ice, the *Krassin* made slow progress. Eventually, the Russian cutter found the two Italian officers who, with Malmgren leading them, had left the others and struck out across the ice floes on May 30. Zappi and Mariano claimed that the big Swede had become increasingly weaker and told them to go on without him. This they had done on June 16, after baptizing the Protestant against his will. They took all of his food with them and alleged to have eaten their last piece of pemmican on June 30. Then they had passively waited thirteen days until the *Krassin* picked them up.

Watching Zappi as he recounted the events, the Russians were disgusted. He appeared not to have a trace of malnutrition and was wearing clothes belonging to his longtime friend

Finn Malmgren, meteorologist on the Norge *and* Italia *flights*

Mariano, who had been found poorly clad, lying with a frostbitten foot in a puddle. Zappi also contradicted his own story by revealing that Malmgren had died while they were with him and that Mariano had "allowed" him to eat the meteorologist's liver.

Enemas given the Italians by the ship's doctor indicated they had not gone without food as long as they claimed. Had they hastened the death of Malmgren? The Swedish press thought so, angrily accusing them of cannibalism.

On the evening of June 12, the *Krassin* reached the remaining five castaways on the ice floe where they had been dumped by the dirigible forty-nine days earlier. Zappi quickly made himself one of the most unlikeable explorers in history. He requested that the two enlisted men, Cecioni and Giuseppe Biagi, not be berthed in the same cabin with the officers, despite their conditions. Cecioni had a fractured leg, it will be recalled, and Biagi was too ill to stand up.

The following day, Zappi rejected a suggestion that the icebreaker search for the crewmen who had been carried off with the remnants of the airship. He was in a hurry to get home; there was no point in wasting time on dead men. Altogether, eight men had been rescued, two were known dead, and twelve were missing, including Amundsen.

While the *Italia* survivors were returning to Kings Bay for transportation home, Amundsen's birthday, July 16, was commemorated in sadness around the world. Six ships at this point were hunting for the famous explorer.

On August 31, ten weeks after the Norseman's disappearance, a fishing boat passing off the Fugloe Islands near Tromsø found a seven-foot float and the fuel tank from a seaplane. When a French mechanic inspected the float, he found a copper plate used to patch a small hole in the bottom of one of the Latham 47's floats. The float and fuel tank appeared to have been screwed off, suggesting they had been used as improvised life rafts. If so, Amundsen and his companions had died fighting for their lives while a huge international effort mostly ignored them and concentrated on rescuing the *Italia* survivors, who were out of danger.

Amundsen, the "last Viking"

The Norwegian Government finally called off the belated hunt for Amundsen on September 6. They assumed he had perished in his beloved Arctic as he had wished—doing something good and useful. But for a long time many Norwegians refused to believe he was dead. He had been missing before; he would return again.

Those who served on Amundsen's expeditions recalled him as straightforward and honorable. He understated his accomplishments, often making them appear easier than they were. A private and reticent man, he never pandered to the public, which undoubtedly restricted his popularity.

"I suppose my discovery of the South Pole will always be regarded by the public as the high point of my life," he rightly had told his friend Ellsworth, "but not with me. My greatest achievement was the Northwest Passage in the *Gjøa*."

With Amundsen went the last of Ellsworth's heroes. "Rated by their influence upon me, the greatest of these was Wyatt Earp, but the one I knew was Amundsen."

9

WYATT EARP

"I am leaving it to younger men," Amundsen had said after the *Norge* flight as he gestured toward Ellsworth. But Ellsworth wasn't ready to take up the mantle. Having realized his lifetime ambition, he thought his days in the polar regions were over. He believed there were "no more worlds to conquer."

He became increasingly restless, however, as he watched others tackling the Antarctic by air. George Wilkins (who had flown across the Arctic with Carl Eielson shortly before the

Italia crash) made the first airplane flight in exploring the bottom of the world. Using a ship-based plane in December of 1928, Wilkins flew six hundred miles across Graham Land (the top of the Antarctic Peninsula). A year later, Richard Byrd and Bernt Balchen flew over the South Pole. Riiser-Larsen, meanwhile, was leading a Norwegian expedition that charted and named the Queen Maud Coast, the last major coastline gap on the Antarctic map. Riiser-Larsen also made a number of flights inland, discovering a vast unseen area that he called Queen Maud Land. Australia's Douglas Mawson was also at work.

Although he was eager for a piece of the action, Ellsworth's only opportunity was to help finance a scheme by Wilkins to cross the Arctic Ocean, this time under it. The Australian wanted to use a submarine to study the continental shelf, ocean currents, the weather, and to establish thirty-two permanent stations on the ice pack. Although he didn't intend to go along, Ellsworth became the scientific adviser as well as the financial backer. An old United States Navy sub was refitted and christened the USS *Nautilus.* Crews were trained and the Wilkins-

Members of Lincoln Ellsworth's first Antarctic Expedition gather in New Zealand before their departure on December 10, 1933. Ellsworth (center, front row) is flanked by Bernt Balchen, his pilot, (left) and George Wilkins, his expedition manager (right).

Ellsworth Trans-Arctic Submarine Expedition set forth from New London, Connecticut, in June of 1931. But due to violent weather and breakdown of equipment, the sub only reached as far as 82°15′ N. Wilkins was somewhat ahead of his time, but he lived to see the nuclear-powered USS *Nautilus* make the underwater crossing in August of 1958.

Before Wilkins returned, Ellsworth received an invitation to join the giant dirigible *Graf Zeppelin* on the inauguration of a summer cruise over the Russian Arctic. Also, the American Geographical Society asked him to go along as their explorer. He snapped up the chance and three weeks later (July 24, 1931) he was aboard the airship.

After traversing Europe, the big blimp departed from Lenningrad on July 26 and crossed the Arctic Circle. It floated over the islands of Novaya Zemlya and Franz Josef Land, east of Spitsbergen. At Hooker Island, the *Graf Zeppelin* hovered low to deliver mail to a Russian icebreaker anchored nearby. Ellsworth noticed someone waving from the boat sent out to pick up the mail. But he didn't recognize the man until he climbed aboard. It was Umberto Nobile.

"I had to look twice to recognize him," Ellsworth wrote. Nobile, who was still searching for possible *Italia* survivors, had aged considerably. In Ellsworth's estimation, the disaster had made him a different man. When the boat departed, Nobile stood unsteadily in the stern, waving good-bye, an unforgettably pathetic figure.

In addition to an exotic adventure, the *Graf Zeppelin* made some significant discoveries. Two islands of the Franz Josef archipelago previously shown on the maps were found not to exist. Nicholas II Land (now Severnaya Zemlya) turned out to be two islands separated by a narrow channel, not one island as believed previously.

But the flight had special significance for Ellsworth beyond its discoveries. The sight of ice and unknown lands fired in him a zeal for exploration he had not felt since meeting Amundsen.

Back in New York, he waited impatiently for Wilkins' return so they could get started on an Antarctic project. Little of the vast southern continent had been seen beyond the coast, except for the corridor from the Ross Sea to the South Pole blazed by Scott, Amundsen, Shackleton, and Byrd. Millions of square miles waited to be unveiled, primarily because of the lack of sites where bases could be set up.

Ellsworth decided that, by using a ship-based airplane, he could cross the unseen interior from the Ross Sea to the Weddell Sea and back again. He roped Wilkins into becoming technical assistant and manager of the expedition. For the 3400-mile flight, he hired Bernt Balchen to pilot the plane, the first of the Gamma class of Northrup monoplanes. The plane, dubbed *Polar Star,* had the longest range of any yet built and was the first American aircraft to be designed with wing flaps to reduce landing speed. It was also equipped with broad, blunt skis, which looked like tennis shoes for a giant.

To carry the expedition south, Ellsworth bought a 400-ton Norwegian herring boat. He had it refitted, still reeking with fish. Sails were added and, among other things, oak planking, covered by a quarter-inch steel plate for icebreaking. He christened the vessel the *Wyatt Earp* in hopes of infusing the entire enterprise with the spirit of the man he considered the bravest.

Since the ten-man Norwegian crew hadn't heard of Marshall Earp, two books about him were carried in the ship's library. The library also had Earp's favorite book, *The Saga of Billy the Kid.* The Norwegians who understood English translated for those who didn't. What they thought about this hasn't been recorded. But Ellsworth could indulge himself because for the first time it was exclusively his expedition.

Before his departure Ellsworth traveled to Europe to brush up on his navigation and aerial photograhy. In Switzerland he met Mary Louise Ulmer, daughter of a Philadelphia industrialist, and they became engaged. They returned to New York, and in the spring of the next year they were married in the Little

Church around the Corner. Ellsworth had just turned fifty-three.

The Ellsworths spent their honeymoon in rainy Christ-church, New Zealand, before the *Wyatt Earp* sailed on December 10, 1933, for the Bay of Whales, Amundsen's landing site for the South Pole. Byrd had recently arrived with his second expedition and established what he called Little America II twelve miles inland.

Three days after their arrival, Ellsworth and Balchen took the *Polar Star* for a 30-minute test over Amundsen's trail to the South Pole. Everything seemed perfect. But early the next morning, shouts rang through the *Wyatt Earp*. Heavy swells were moving out from under the ice face, cracking the sea ice. The bay had suddenly become a grinding mass of ice floes. On one chunk the *Polar Star* was marooned temporarily; then the floe split and the airplane dropped into the crack. Only its wings were keeping the $37,000 investment out of the water.

Since the plane could no longer fly, they hoisted it aboard and headed back to New Zealand.

Ellsworth, however, was undeterred. He regrouped, deciding to make a one-way flight across the Antarctic continent from the Antarctic Peninsula. Located farther north, the peninsula could be reached earlier in the season than the Bay of Whales because the summer thaw occurs sooner there. This would enable the expedition to have more time.

The *Wyatt Earp* sailed from New Zealand on September 19, 1934. Seventeen men were on board, with enough food for two years, the repaired *Polar Star,* and a hold full of rats.

The doctor, who had been on the Byrd Expedition to Little America, was seasick during the entire voyage. He lay in his bunk with his cap pulled down over his eyes.

How had he managed the trip with Byrd? Ellsworth asked him.

"I don't know," he moaned. "I only remember the highlights."

Ellsworth (right) and Bernt Balchen in New Zealand with the Wyatt Earp *in the background.*

Was this doctor going to be another dud? Ellsworth worried. During the first expedition, Balchen had developed appendicitis, and the ship was forced to put in at Cape Town, South Africa, for the operation. Although the expedition doctor was only observing, he fainted at the sight of the incision. Later, in the Ross Sea, when Ellsworth asked for formalin with which to preserve some fish specimens, the doctor had given him a handful of mothballs.

In October the expedition reached Deception Island. The island seemed ideal. It was located off the western coast of the peninsula—along the route Amundsen had sailed in the *Belgica* thirty-six years earlier. In addition to shelter provided by an abandoned Norwegian whaling factory, the bay ice looked suitable for a runway. Only the weather remained incalculable. It proved to be intractable as well. Rain, sleet, gale-force winds, and snow squalls kept Ellsworth and Balchen from getting off the ground. Then a connecting rod broke, and the *Wyatt Earp* had to be sent to fetch a replacement part from Chile.

Ellsworth, Balchen, and three others stayed behind in the whaling factory sheds. The leader had time to study a nearby rookery of Adélie penguins, which he called a "daffy race." He tried eating the eggs, which weren't bad in omelets. But boiled! "Ye Gods! Tough as rubber balls and fishy besides!" Amundsen no doubt would have relished them.

By the time the *Wyatt Earp* returned, the temperature had become so mild that most of the snow had disappeared. The expedition was compelled to search for a new base. They sailed south, as if following the ghost of the young Amundsen, but the pack ice forced them to retreat northward. Eventually, the explorers stopped at Snow Hill Island on the eastern side of the peninsula. The famous Nordenskjöld Expedition had been stranded here from February of 1902 until December of 1903. Despite nearly starving to death, the Swedes had collected fossils and rock specimens that for the first time revealed the peninsula to be an extension of the South American Andes. The danger at Snow Hill Island was obvious, but Ellsworth planned to be out of there before the pack ice had a chance to repeat its performance.

While the *Polar Star* was being assembled, lowered, and taxied up a glacier to a snowfield, Ellsworth crossed the island to Nordenskjöld's hut. No one had been there since the occupants had been rescued thirty-one years before. Ellsworth found the mummies of three white sledge dogs in front of the hut where they had fallen when shot. Frozen cases of food were piled against the cabin. Ellsworth sampled the chocolate, which tasted good as new, but neither he nor his companions were later willing to try the vintage fish.

Inside the hut were more artifacts, all in an excellent state of preservation. The place was neat. The clock on the wall had stopped at three o'clock. Ellsworth salvaged some of the relics and presented them to the American Museum of Natural History. The most curious object in the hut was a cone-shaped block of blue ice in the middle of the room. No one could imagine how the ice could have been formed in such a particular way. Ellsworth later met the botantist of the Nordenskjöld Expedition who explained, "We always did mean to mend that leak in the roof." The mysterious ice block represented thirty-one years of dripping.

On December 18, the Ellsworth expedition got its first entirely clear day after two months in the Antarctic. The leader and Balchen took off in the *Polar Star* and flew to the southern end of the Nordenskjöld Coast before returning. The midnight sun, perched on the southern horizon, tinted the ice-covered Weddell Sea with a rosy light in which the flat-topped icebergs "gleamed like rubies." The round trip took two and one-half hours.

Conditions were so good that the two were convinced they would be winging toward Little America the next day. But, as frequently happens in the Antarctic, the weather changed. Snow squalls screamed across the sea and persisted with overcast skies until the end of the month.

Hut built by the stranded Nordenskjöld Expedition on Snow Hill Island in 1902

The situation appeared hopeless by January 3. The expedition began to pack up. But when they went ashore to dig out the plane, Ellsworth was seized with an impulse.

"Let's make a try! What do you say?" he asked Balchen.

"All right," the pilot agreed.

After a hot meal, they climbed aboard the *Polar Star* and shot down the icy grade in a flurry of snow. They circled the ship and headed south. Ellsworth busied himself taking notes of landmarks. At one point, he looked up and discovered their direction had changed. They were heading back!

He shouted at Balchen for an explanation.

"Bad weather," came the Norwegian's laconic response.

Balchen believed a storm was threatening in the distance, although the sun was shining on either side of the small, dark formation. Ellsworth was convinced they could have gotten through and that Balchen didn't want to make the flight unless the weather was perfect. An entirely clear day was as rare as rain in the Antarctic!

They bumped down on Snow Hill Island after covering four hundred miles. When they came to a stop, Ellsworth jumped out and floundered off through the snow to the ship. His feelings didn't need an interpreter.

Wilkins, who had climbed up to meet them, asked Balchen what had happened.

"Ellsworth can commit suicide if he likes," the pilot said, "but he can't take me with him."

Ellsworth had to be satisified with the discovery of five islands, five fjords, and several mountain peaks on the eastern rim of the peninsula. It was time to head for home.

Steaming north, the *Wyatt Earp* encountered such heavy ice that it had to retreat sixty miles. While the explorers waited for the wind to move the ice out of their way, the Antarctic night crept toward them. Darkness increased to four hours each day. Would they face the same fate as the *Belgica?*

After six days, the *Wyatt Earp* got a start north again, but soon came to a standstill. The relentless pack ice began pressing around the ship, threatening to smash it against the shore. Working furiously throughout the night, the men hurried to prepare to abandon ship.

Early in the morning the wind shifted. Taking advantage of the opening leads, the *Wyatt Earp* pushed its way slowly northward again. It was touch and go, but eventually the ship broke through the ice into the Atlantic. Yet the warmer weather brought on a new problem. Rats.

The rat colony picked up in New Zealand had multiplied in the hold. Rats began swarming all over the ship, killing and eating one of the cats on board. One morning Ellsworth woke to see

The Wyatt Earp *crew feared being caught in the Antarctic ice pack.*

a huge rat clinging to the ceiling of his cabin. That was enough. Declaring war, the crew took sticks and killed "169 on deck and dozens below decks." The rats had eaten all the leather they could find, including the men's mukluk boots and the webbing out of their snowshoes.

10

THIRD TIME LUCKY

As Ellsworth headed home, he believed the difficulties of a transantarctic flight were insurmountable. The project, after two failures, had become as frustrating as Amundsen's attempts to drift across the Arctic in the *Maud*.

But the wealthy American couldn't put the mocking beauty of the Antarctic out of his mind. He was plagued by the memory of "icy land and icy sea crowded with flat-topped bergs, delicately purple at noon, liquid gold when the sun declined to its midnight position."

Ellsworth couldn't forget the beauty of the Antarctic.

In New York, the head of the North American Newspaper Alliance advised him, "What do you want to go back there for, Ellsworth? You'll lose your life. Try something else—something easier." The advice was just what Ellsworth needed. It roused his pioneering spirit, the spirit of Wyatt Earp that was never daunted by overwhelming odds.

He determined to make a third try. He hired two Canadian Airways pilots with experience flying in the Arctic: Herbert Hollick-Kenyon as pilot and J. H. Lymburner as backup. They joined Ellsworth and the rest of the crew in Montevideo, Uruguay, where the ship was moored. The expedition sailed south in October of 1935.

Ellsworth had written to Byrd asking if he had left any usable food at Little America II. The leader was taking precautions in case the *Wyatt Earp* had trouble getting through the ice pack to rescue him and Hollick-Kenyon at the end of their flight.

Ellsworth received Byrd's answer at a refueling stop in Chile. It had been written six months earlier and for some reason hadn't been sent sooner. Byrd merely informed him of the disposition of the gasoline and oil that Ellsworth had shipped to Little America with Byrd the preceding year. But Byrd promised a later message about the food supplies. Considering the help given by Amundsen and Ellsworth to Byrd before his North Pole flight, Ellsworth must have been more than a little piqued. But he made no comment.

During the five-day voyage south, the new ship's doctor lived up to the regrettable reputation of his predecessors. One day in the mess, the flag-waving doctor accused the entire Norwegian breed of clannishness. That was too much for the Norwegian crew. With one blow the second mate decked the doctor. Although the mate apologized later, the physician wouldn't listen. The next morning he posted a notice: "During the rest of the voyage I will give no professional services to the members of this expedition."

At Dundee Island, near Deception Island, the explorers discovered an ideal flying base: large sweeps of hard snow. There was also a diversion on the bay ice: Weddell seals so tame they wouldn't move out of the way. They enjoyed having their sides scratched with sticks, rolling over on their backs like contented kittens.

The *Polar Star* was assembled and test flown. But above-freezing temperatures soon made the runway snow wet and sticky, preventing the heavily loaded plane from getting enough speed for takeoff. Knowing the situation would soon change, they continued with preparations. Since Byrd had not been heard from, they decided to settle for seals and penguins, if necessary, when they reached the Bay of Whales.

Ellsworth and Hollick-Kenyon finally got airborne on November 21. In addition to survival gear, Ellsworth carried along the American flag and various club pennants, a Micky Mouse replica, and an 1849 ox shoe he had found in Death Valley. He

172

The Polar Star *is hoisted onto the ice barrier from the* Wyatt Earp.

also took his most treasured mementos: Wyatt Earp's cartridge belt and the gold wedding band that Mrs. Earp had given him in memory of her husband.

The *Polar Star* flew along the eastern coast of the peninsula. By noon, the explorers were over unknown territory. Crossing the base of the peninsula, they encountered a new mountain range, which Ellsworth named the Eternity Range because of the sublimity of the silent peaks. The three central summits he called Faith, Hope, and Charity.

But gale-force winds soon forced them back toward Dundee Island. Hollick-Kenyon, resigned to the situation, passed Ellsworth a note.

"I've just had lunch. Have you?"

Lunch! How could anyone think about eating at such a time?

Their setback, however, was only temporary. The next day weather conditions were perfect and they were off again. Taking out his camera, Ellsworth photographed the Eternity Mountain Range as they flew past. Three hours later, the mountains gave way to a vast ice plateau, pierced only by a few nunataks, or mountain peaks.

Everything seemed to be right for success. Then, about 950 miles from their destination, the pilot passed a distressing note to Ellsworth:

"Transmitter out of action. What shall we do?"

Keep going, was Ellsworth's response. He didn't want to set down before they reached their first objective—80° W longitude.

Although their radio had quit during a report of excellent flying conditions, rescue attempts were immediately organized in the United States and Australia. Veteran explorers, including Byrd, voiced confidence, but the newspapers sensationalized the story. THE ILL-FATED ELLSWORTH FLIGHT screamed across front pages.

Meanwhile, the *Polar Star* droned on nearly a mile above an uninterrupted prairie of snow. There were no landmarks to help the two aviators determine drift or ground speed. But after about another one hundred miles, they discovered a solitary little mountain range. Ellsworth called it the Sentinel Range and the central peak he named Mount Mary Louise Ulmer for his wife. (The range today is known as the Ellsworth Mountains.)

Mirages began to play with them as they continued. Water appeared where there was none. Pitfalls and other obstacles proved to be nonexistent. They had been in the air for fourteen hours. Seeing a stretch of hard-packed snow, they decided to set down. This surface certainly wasn't deceptive. The landing was so hard that the skis made little impression, and Ellsworth thought his teeth would go through his head. Worse, the fuse-

OPPOSITE: *Ellsworth's flights across Antarctica*

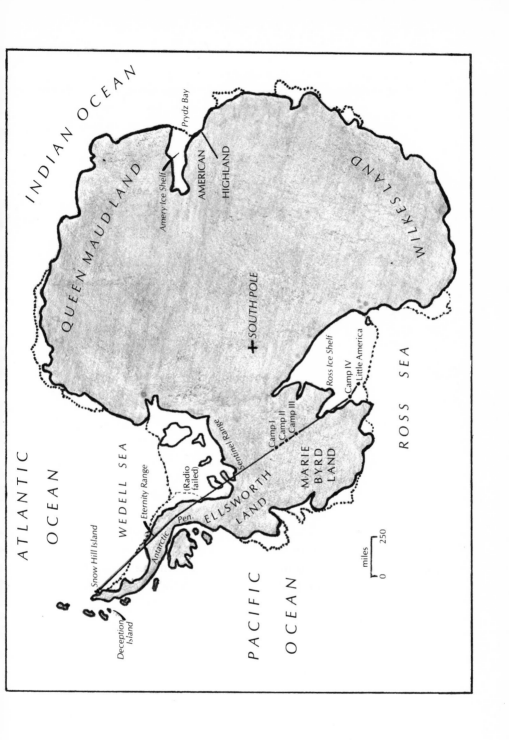

lage crumpled, although the plane was still flyable.

When Ellsworth tried to use the sextant to take position readings, he found that the instrument wasn't working properly. He was compelled to estimate their position—at what became Camp I—450 miles south of the coast, 650 miles north of the pole, and 670 miles east of Little America II. Whatever their exact position, they had reached one of the last unclaimed lands in the world. Raising the flag, Ellsworth named the area for his father and the plateau for Hollick-Kenyon.

When they headed off nineteen hours later (November 24), thickening weather forced them to land after only thirty minutes. Here, at Camp II, they tried for three days to get a reading of their position. But the weather never cleared sufficiently. With only a rough idea of their whereabouts, they took off in the direction they hoped was Little America II.

This time they were forced down after fifty minutes. A storm was building. Quickly they pitched a tent as the blizzard struck, stalling them for seven days. At times, the force of the wind seemed about to blow away the tent and its two occupants, but the tent pegs had frozen firmly in the snow.

Whenever the wind slackened, the men cut snow blocks and worked on a wall to help shelter the tent. Despite this barricade, the gusts shook the canvas, knocking them about. They would slide over nearly on top of each other as they tried to rest and sleep at Camp III.

After three days, they crawled out of the tent to find the plane nearly buried in snowdrifts. The snow had worked its way into the plane as well. Using a bucket and a mug, it took Ellsworth a day just to scoop out the inside of the tail. Ellsworth lost the feeling in his left foot while he worked to free the plane, but he dismissed the problem as being due to the cold.

One benefit of the storm was that Ellsworth had time to find out what was wrong with the sextant—a loose index lock nut. With the sextant working properly, they could get a better fix on their position. To their disappointment, they were still more than five hundred miles from the Bay of Whales.

176

One of the Antarctic mountain summits seen by Lincoln Ellsworth during his transantarctic flight

Hollick-Kenyon managed to repair their radio set and strung an antenna on bamboo poles. Using a portable generator, he flashed their position before the set went dead. Although they were in no immediate danger, they worried that the outside world might fear they were in trouble.

They carried three months' emergency food rations on the plane, but they ate only twice a day and were never hungry. Food didn't seem important. Their interest was directed toward getting out of that hole.

That night it snowed heavily and they had to dig out the plane again. When they had finished and were ready to take off, another storm broke, forcing them to set up Camp III once more.

Hollick-Kenyon was a quiet man. His silences, Ellsworth said, made even the Norwegians seem talkative. During the time they spent on the continent, he offered only two remarks beyond comments pertaining to work. That night in the tent he spoke for both of them when he said, "Maybe this is all meant to try us out." Both men knew their predicament. If they

177

couldn't get airborne, they would have to man-haul their supplies 450 miles to the coast.

In the morning, December 4, the two intrepid explorers hurriedly set off despite threatening skies. But luck was with them. The skies cleared as they headed into Marie Byrd Land, which Byrd had flown over earlier. Below them, the surface began dropping in elevation, falling away in great undulations. At the same time, great crevasses began to appear, warning the aviators they couldn't set down in that area.

They found a safe-looking place four hours later and landed to make a careful check of their position and fuel tanks. This, Camp IV, placed them 125 miles from Little America II. They had left the high plateau region and were now on the Ross Ice Shelf. The wind was calm. The crystals of snow sparkled like jewels.

Ellsworth rejoiced. Once more it was good to be alive!

The next morning, after an hour in the air, they sighted the Ross Sea. The water appeared slate colored, almost black in comparison to the white expanse they had seen for days. Hollick-Kenyon turned and looked at Ellsworth, but neither could think of anything to say on the historic occasion. They had made the first flight across the Antarctic Continent and claimed a large chunk for the United States. And they had made it just in time. A little later their fuel ran out, and the *Polar Star* glided to the surface like a tired bird come home to rest.

They secured the plane in a trench and set out on snowshoes for Little America II. They knew it couldn't be too far from them; actually it was buried in the snow sixteen miles away. They set out for it several times, only to be forced by the difficult terrain to return to the plane. Once what they believed to be Byrd's camp turned out to be only pressure ridges of upended ice.

On December 9, they packed a sledge with provisions and again began marching toward the Bay of Whales. Hopefully from that position they could locate the covered outpost. As they labored across the sastrugi, the aviators got a taste of the terrible struggle of Scott and his party. Hollick-Kenyon wanted to jettison some of the load, but Ellsworth wouldn't allow it. If they became lost, they would need everything.

Complicating their ordeal, a heavy fog drifted in. Sometimes the fog was so thick they couldn't see more than a few yards ahead. At other times the sun filtered through—a high overhead December sun that filled the air with a weird light at midnight.

They began to feel a loss of equilibrium as they pressed on. Illusions toyed with them, such as holes appearing in the surface ahead and the sensation that they were traveling downhill. Aware they were developing "polar nerves," they didn't speak to one another. Ellsworth had to endure an added burden. His left foot had remained numb. He finally examined it one evening in the tent while the pilot was cooking. It was a shock. His entire foot looked like one large water blister. He quickly put on his socks and boot. He said nothing because nothing could be done. But when dinner was served, he had lost his appetite.

On the sixth day after leaving the plane, December 15, they thought they heard a storm beyond a ridge ahead of them. Un-

An example of rugged Antarctic terrain

strapping the sledge harness, they climbed the ridge and got quite a surprise. Two hundred feet straight down was the black tumbling water of the Ross Sea. They beat a hasty retreat, realizing what they had thought to be wind and thunder were waves crashing against the cliff of ice.

Although they had found the sea, they still didn't know in which direction to find Little America II. All they could do was guess. They picked west.

That afternoon, they crested a long sastrugi and saw the most desolate remains of past habitation Ellsworth had ever beheld. Only a sparse thicket of masts, poles, stovepipes, and guy wires protruded above the snow where the busy American camp once had been located.

Digging near a stovepipe, they found a glass skylight, which they broke through, landing in the abandoned radio shack. Ellsworth produced two small bottles of brandy from his pack, and they celebrated. They had sledged more than one hundred miles to find the outpost, directly located only sixteen miles from the plane.

After searching through the tunnels connecting all of the buildings, they found coal for the stove and enough food to live on for three months. They were safe in quarters fifteen feet below the snow. Their only enemy was the insidious destructive force of isolation—boredom.

Model of Little America, Richard Byrd's camp, which Ellsworth

Their daily routine consisted of keeping watch for the *Wyatt Earp* to arrive in the bay and hunting for food. To conserve coal, they initially spent most of their time, usually fifteen hours a day, in their sleeping bags. But after two weeks they couldn't tolerate so much sack time.

The monotony quickly became oppressive for Ellsworth, who had left his glasses on the plane. As a result, he had great difficulty reading and writing. One eventless evening, Ellsworth touched a wad of chewing gum stuck underneath the bed frame. For two days he debated chewing it, just to have something different to do. But then Hollick-Kenyon discovered two packs of gum and the historic wad remained preserved on the bed frame.

As the days dragged by, Ellsworth claimed he would have paid a thousand dollars for his glasses. The plane was not far away, but he feared they would become lost if they attempted to find it. So Ellsworth waited, becoming increasingly edgy as his companion's habits became increasingly irritating. Unable to read, Ellsworth would be forced to listen to Hollick-Kenyon's gurgling pipe as the pilot "lost" himself in one detective story after another.

Ellsworth plotted revenge similar to the way in which he had eaten his biscuits after Feucht in the Arctic. He convinced Hollick-Kenyon that they had lost track of the date. It was December 24, not December 23. As a result, they celebrated Christmas

and Hollick-Kenyon used after their historic flight

the next day. But Ellsworth's trick was exposed a day later by a total eclipse of the sun. The pilot knew the unusual event was expected on Christmas afternoon of that year.

The condition of Ellsworth's foot, meanwhile, had steadily deteriorated. Despite swelling and red streaks up his leg, he refused to admit it was becoming gangrenous. He soon developed a fever and was forced to stay in bed. He told Hollick-Kenyon he was resting his leg to let it heal. They had been at Little America II one month, although it seemed much longer.

Despite his condition, Ellsworth struggled to maintain his diary. On January 15, he noticed that something dropped on the skylight. He imagined it was a penguin. "The first penguins this year at the Bay of Whales," he entered in his diary. "One flopped on the skylight as I lay writing."

But it had not been a penguin. A note with a parcel of food had been parachuted from an airplane searching for them. The plane had come from the British Royal Antarctic Research Society's ship, *Discovery II,* which had been sent by the Australian Government to rescue them. Four days later, the *Wyatt Earp* arrived, several days ahead of schedule, and Ellsworth's foot was attended to.

Although he was grateful to the Australians for sending the *Discovery II,* Ellsworth was not pleased to see the ship. He hadn't asked for help and didn't need any. He feared that the news media would give the world the impression he had to be rescued. His fears were more than justified. In addition to saying he needed to be rescued, some of the news media charged that he had deliberately maintained radio silence in order to generate more publicity for himself.

Ellsworth argued that such accusations were wrong. Wilkins, who was directing operations from the *Wyatt Earp,* had not been concerned about the safety of the two explorers and the loss of radio contact. Two days after they'd taken off, Wilkins had heard from the Byrd Expedition about the food left behind. There were caches near Little America II and ample food and coal in the tunnels of the camp itself. Wilkins was so confident all was proceeding according to plan that he'd radioed the Australian Government and informed them that their rescue attempt was not needed. The *Wyatt Earp,* he assured them, would be at the Bay of Whales on schedule to make the pick up.

Despite the carping, Ellsworth received a resounding welcome first in Australia and then in the United States. Congress voted Ellsworth a special gold medal for "claiming on behalf of the United States approximately three hundred and fifty thousand square miles of land in Antarctica . . . representing the last unclaimed territory in the world. . . ."

Ellsworth had also made a very important contribution to the future of polar exploration. He and Hollick-Kenyon had demonstrated that landings could be made and bases established in the Antarctic interior.

11

FINAL VISTAS

Restlessness nagged at Ellsworth. Despite his crowning achievement, he longed for another unseen vista. At fifty-eight, he had no intention of retiring, even though an old pro like Amundsen had bowed out at fifty-four. Since more information was needed on what the interior of Antarctica looked like, he turned his attention south once again.

One sizeable area on the Indian Ocean side of the continent remained unexplored. Ellsworth decided to make a flight across it to the Bay of Whales, a 2000-mile trip.

He set forth in the fall of 1938 for his last hurrah. But the pack ice, extending north 813 miles, kept the *Wyatt Earp* from reaching the continent in time to complete the expedition's goal. It was too late in the season to attempt the crossing. Fortunately Ellsworth recognized the situation as hopeless. He had received his kudos and wasn't tempted to make a dangerous flight to prove himself as Amundsen had done.

With Lymburner, his backup pilot from the 1935 expedition, Ellsworth was able to get in one short flight. On January 11, 1939, the pair took off from Prydz Bay and flew two hundred miles inland. They looked down from 4500 feet to see a vast wind-rifled desert, unblemished white stretching to the horizon. It looked so peaceful in the mellowing glow of a low western sun. It was a new and a last horizon.

Using the altimeter, Ellsworth judged the area, about the size of Nebraska, to be 1500 feet above sea level and gently rising toward the south. He dropped the American flag and a message in a tube claiming the region, called the American Highland, for the United States.

Although men from Australia, Germany, and Norway had previously explored the coastline, Ellsworth was the first to see the interior of this side of the continent. Today, Australia claims the territory that includes the American Highland. (Ellsworth Land remains unclaimed on the other side of the continent.) Under the Antarctic Treaty, the major nations of the world have agreed to postpone the question of territorial ownership in Antarctica so that every country can have access to the continent for scientific research. The United States has made no claims, does not recognize claims of others, and reserves the right to make claims in the future based on the explorations of its citizens, such as Lincoln Ellsworth.

Later in 1939, Ellsworth fell down a cliff in the Grand Canyon, which he liked to visit every summer if possible, and suffered a permanent head injury. He died on May 26, 1951, in New York City, following a heart attack.

Wilkins said that Ellsworth, like a boy, loved notoriety. If so, Ellsworth's fame was short lived. He never became as celebrated as his idols, Wyatt Earp and Roald Amundsen. A permanent exhibit has been devoted to Ellsworth in the American Museum of Natural History, although one suspects this is due to his long association with the museum and his contributions to it, as much as it is because of his place in history. Except for that, however, Ellsworth has joined the ranks of virtually forgotten explorers. Few books have been devoted to his work, whereas Amundsen has been the subject of many, primarily because of the race to the South Pole.

Amundsen's greater accomplishments, of course, deserve more attention. Yet a prejudice seems to exist against Ellsworth. Why? Maybe it is because some people viewed him as a wealthy adventure-hound who bought his way onto expeditions. True, it was Ellsworth's money that enabled Amundsen to continue his career and to regain his self-respect at a time when his fortunes had reached bedrock. But that in itself would have been a significant contribution.

Ellsworth, however, was far more than simply Amundsen's benefactor. Ellsworth's financial assistance did make possible the flights of 1925 and 1926, Amundsen said. But that was not the extent of his contributions. As the Norwegian put it: "Ellsworth and I had been congenial companions in danger and in achievement. I was delighted to share the national honours with my beloved American friend."

Amundsen's respect for his American friend is evident when he wrote that Ellsworth had gone to Norway a month before the *Norge* flight to perfect his navigational ability. But then when he arrived in Spitsbergen and found that those duties already had been assigned to Riiser-Larsen, "Ellsworth was too large spirited to interfere."

After the *Norge* Expedition, when Nobile tried to split up the two leaders, Amundsen said that the Italian had misjudged Ellsworth's character. "He is a gentleman as well as a loyal friend and a clean sportsman."

Amundsen and Ellsworth, partners in search of new frontiers

Ellsworth also made his own contributions, whether it was navigating, studying atmospheric electricity, or providing geographical data. He was more than patron and intimate friend. Ellsworth was an explorer in his own right. His Antarctic flights may be the basis for claims by the United States to large areas of Antarctica that have increasing political and mineral importance.

Amundsen defined exploring as a "highly technical and serious profession, calling for laborious years of physical and mental preparation." The objective was to seek facts about the unknown, not "the mere thrills of the adventurer and the cheap, brief fame of charlatans and notoriety seekers." Amundsen would have characterized Nobile in such terms, but not Ellsworth, even though the sentimental Ellsworth was impressed by his own accomplishments.

Although he was reticent about revealing his emotions, Amundsen appears to have enjoyed the planning and execution of an expedition rather than the honors that followed. He was a no-nonsense, dedicated, professional explorer—the explorer's explorer. He enjoyed the ordeal of the challenge, like an individual who is happiest while striving for his goal. Perhaps it can be said that Amundsen enjoyed the hardship, where Ellsworth endured the hardship for the reward of accomplishment. Adventure may not have been their primary objective, but it certainly was a motivating force for both of them.

It is difficult to assess either explorer because most personal conflict has been eradicated from their diaries and journals. When an expedition was over, they felt that any unpleasantness should be forgotten (with the exception of Nobile.) The Polar Legion they established was a tight-knit club indeed. But one thing is evident—Amundsen and Ellsworth got along remarkably well. Not only were they ideal partners, but they appeared to be genuinely fond of one another—two kindred spirits brought together by the lure of the unknown.

BIBLIOGRAPHY

Amundsen, Roald. *My Life as an Explorer*. Garden City, New York: Doubleday, Doran, 1928.

————. *The Northwest Passage*. London: Constable, 1908.

————. *The South Pole*. London: John Murray, 1912.

Amundsen, Roald and Ellsworth, Lincoln. *First Crossing of the Polar Sea*. New York: Doran, 1927.

————. *Our Polar Flight*. New York: Dodd, Mead, 1925.

Byrd, Richard E. *Skyward*. New York: Putnam's Sons, 1928.

Cook, Frederick A. "Two Thousand Miles in the Antarctic Ice." *McClure's Magazine*, Vol. XIV, Nov. 1899.

Ellsworth, Lincoln. *Beyond Horizons*. Garden City, New York: Doubleday, Doran, 1937.

————. *Exploring Today*. New York: Dodd, Mead, 1935.

————. *Search*. New York: Brewer, Warren, & Putnam, 1932.

Giudici, Davide. *The Tragedy of the Italia. With the Rescuers to the Red Tent*. New York: Appleton, 1929.

Hanssen, Helmer. *Voyages of a Modern Viking*. London: Routledge, 1936.

Huntford, Roland. *Scott and Amundsen*. New York: Putnam's Sons, 1980.

Montague, Richard. *Oceans, Poles, and Airmen*. New York: Random House, 1971.

Nobile, Umberto. *My Polar Flights*. New York: Putnam's Sons, 1961.

Partridge, Bellamy. *Amundsen*. London: Robert Hale, 1953.

Quartermain, L. B. *South to the Pole*. London: Oxford University Press, 1967.

Scott, Captain Robert F. *Scott's Last Expedition*. New York: Dodd, Mead, 1913.

Shackleton, Ernest. *The Heart of the Antarctic*. London: Heinemann, 1909.

Simmons, George. *Target: Arctic*. Philadelphia: Chilton, 1965.

Turley, Charles. *Roald Amundsen, Explorer*. London: Methuen, 1935.

INDEX

190